THE ROOT *of* ALL FEAR

How Uncovering the Lies You Believe About God Sets You Free from Anxiety

DAWN ISLER COX

LUCIDBOOKS

The Root of All Fear: How Uncovering the Lies You Believe About God Sets You Free from Anxiety

Published by Lucid Books in Houston, TX
www.LucidBooks.com

Paperback ISBN: 978-1-63296-970-5
eISBN: 978-1-63296-971-2

Special Sales: Most Lucid Books titles are available in special quantity discounts. Custom imprinting or excerpting can also be done to fit special needs. Contact Lucid Books at Info@LucidBooks.com

For Paul,
who has walked beside me through
every Berry Bush excavation,
never once setting down his shovel.
Thank you for believing in me!

CONTENTS

Part III
Your Anxiety Action Plan

Part IV
The Berry Bush

Part V
How to Live Out the Truth Tree

SPECIAL THANKS

To Shaelyn Xi: Thank you for your beautiful illustrations that captured the Berry Bush and the Truth Tree with such creativity and care.

To Benjamin: Thank you for teaching me so much about the root of fear. Your example of perseverance and courage to share your story strengthened this book in ways you may never fully know.

To Paul, Sam, Caroline, Joe, Annabelle, Becky, and Mom: Thank you for standing with me when I felt like giving up, for allowing your stories to become part of these pages, and for reading and listening through every chapter. Your encouragement has carried me.

To Robin MacKinnon: Thank you. If you hadn't invited me to speak at the women's retreat, I would never have heard about a poisonous berry bush. Dreaming, praying, and brainstorming together with you, Christian, and Paul brought the *Berry Bush and the Truth Tree* to life. Thank you for believing in me and spurring me on in my faith.

INTRODUCTION

Uprooting anxiety? Is that possible? Our relationship with anxiety runs so deep that it is hard to imagine being able to reach down far enough to find the deepest of its roots and begin to remove it, but that is what this book is all about. This is an invitation to uproot anxiety, break the thought cycle, and discover the origin of all our lies.

Early one morning, I took a walk along a trail near my home. As I strolled along, I glanced into the woods and was struck by the beauty of a large, deep green bush with plump red berries on it. I had never seen a bush quite like this, and I couldn't resist getting a closer look, so I left the trail to examine it. As I gazed up at the giant leafy shrub, I wondered at its enormous size. At first, it seemed like just one bush, but up close, it was clear there were several bushes growing close together, intertwining with each other's branches. Gleaming in the early morning sun, the crimson berries hung off the limbs in little clusters. There were so many! I doubted the berries were edible, but they looked so inviting. As I moved to get a closer look, my foot caught, and I stumbled on a portion of the root. I stayed there on the ground for some time, staring at that gnarly fibrous root, considering how much of it was underneath the surface. The roots are hidden, but they are the most crucial part of the plant. They sustain it. Those unseen roots feed and support the bush, allowing it to grow to a tremendous size. I wondered what was underneath this poisonous berry bush.

I'm generally not so inquisitive about nature, but the correlation between a poisonous berry bush and my own thought life seemed so apparent to me. If my thought life is like a poisonous berry bush full of worries and fears, then that means I have my own gnarly fibrous roots that are spoon-feeding me anxiety. These roots are nurturing my worries and supporting my fears. This root system is feeding my thoughts poison. Each poisonous berry on my bush represents a worry or fear that is sustained by lies. There are lots of lies underneath, joining the root system; however, they all feed one big, terrible root that lies beneath, hidden and unacknowledged. This is the lie that lies underneath all our fears. This is the lie that is the origin of all our lies.

This book is the journey I am on, even now, of digging up roots and locating my lie underneath. My journey began many years ago when I read the book *Lies Women Believe* by Nancy DeMoss Wolgemuth. In it, she uses an illustration about a poisonous berry bush, comparing the berries to the lies women believe. She shares how important it is not just to pick the berries off, but to permanently get rid of them by pulling the bush out from the roots.[1] That image stirred a new curiosity in me. I began seeing my fears as poisonous berries on a dangerous bush and felt compelled to uncover my own berries and dig them out once and for all. The Berry Bush is where I set out on my trek to find a tool that would help me finally take my thoughts captive. Excavating these roots led me to realize that all the lies I had been telling myself came from one source—a lie about the character of God. To stop listening to my lies, I would need to discover the lie beneath my lies.

This is not a self-help book advising you to just stop believing lies and believe in yourself. This is not a book on how to improve your thought life and be more positive. This is a book about God and His character. The goal of this book is to take you, the reader, to the place where you can discover and excavate root lies you are believing about God.

I have written this book for anyone who, like me, understands that we believe lies and wants to stop. We wish we could replace them with truth, but we struggle to know how to do that. I use the word *struggle* because it's truly a wrestling match with yourself and your thought process to figure out how to stop believing the lies and living with the fears they cause. Those fears keep coming back, and the lies continue to have a voice in our heads. I have written this book because after sharing the idea of the Berry Bush with others, many of them tell me that they find freedom using this tool. That is my hope for you. That once you discover your root lie, you will see how it has been nourishing all your poisonous berries. I think of them as barrier berries, they barricade us from complete communion with God. When we realize that these barrier berries are lies, we will comprehend the magnitude of their impact. These barrier berries govern our thoughts, dictating how we feel, how we behave, and what we believe. Once we recognize our barrier berries, we are empowered, and that truth enables us to reach down deep to the lie underneath. Then we can name that root lie, grab it tight, rip it up, and replace it with the root of truth.

We will begin the book by considering how our thoughts affect everything about us: our mood, how we view ourselves, respond to others, and how we perceive the world. My hope is that by the time you finish this book, you'll see that everything in life flows from the truth of God's character. His goodness, trustworthiness, love, acceptance, and sovereignty will overflow into your thoughts, words, attitudes, and actions. I am trusting God to use this book in your life, opening your eyes and heart to deeper peace and a fuller freedom with Him than you've ever known. I am praying that as you read these pages, God will use the Berry Bush to reveal any barrier that exists between you and Him. I wrote these pages with the expectation that they would provide you with a practical tool to help you identify the lies beneath your fears, expose any unbelief, and destroy whatever barriers that exist between you and God. My prayer is that your thoughts will transform, and you will experience His freedom as you daily live out your Truth Tree.

PART I

THE LIE UNDERNEATH

Chapter 1

THE LIES OF MY FEARS

Not again! I have been here before. I've tried to put this thought out of my head, ignore it, and move on, but here I am once more. My nerves are on edge. My mind is racing. A wave of nausea comes over me. The dread is growing within me, distorting my ability to be rational. My stomach churns. My breathing grows shallow, and irritability courses throughout my body. Without even realizing it, I am allowing that thought to hijack my day, affecting my thoughts, feelings, and actions. It starts small, a voice in my head, an idea, a lie.

I heard a song today that really resonated with me. It is a country song called "Lies of My Fears." [1] It caught my attention when I recognized my own predicament in the singer's story—letting the voice in my head push me around. I turned up the volume as I heard the singer confidently declare that she would not listen to the lies of her fears, and I wondered is it possible not to listen to the lies of my fears? I have tried not to give them any attention, but I continue to struggle. It seems that I am all ears when it comes to the lies of my fears. As I sat in the pew one Sunday morning, listening to another sermon about lies. I felt as if God was winking and nodding at me to listen up. I am amazed at how He continues to point out the impact of lies on my thought life. From what I see on my phone, listen to, the books I pick up, my conversations with friends, and now one more sermon all are telling me to stop believing lies and replace them with truth. I agree–Yes! I want to change, not worry, and not live in negativity. I want to stop being anxious and just believe. . . . That sounds amazing! But how do I do that? I feel like I am trapped in the movie *Groundhog Day.*[2] I am re-living my unbelief over and over again each day. I am caught, wanting to believe the truth that I know in my head, but unable to live it out.

I have consumed hundreds of podcasts, audiobooks, and sermons about how to stop believing lies and replace them with truth. They discuss how lies are hidden beneath the surface of our thoughts. They say we need to see how our thoughts are rooted in a lie and then replace that lie with the truth. It sounds so simple, but I continue to wrestle with lies and allow the anxiety they create to distract, disillusion, and disable me. These lies of my fears are pushing me around in my head, and I know it, but knowing they are lies has not caused me to stop ruminating over them, allowing them to affect my thoughts, feelings, and behavior. Can you relate? Are there fears that are pushing you around? Are there lies that are strong-arming your emotions and behavior, compelling you to listen? Are they persuading you to keep thinking about them despite all your efforts to stop believing lies and replace them with the truth?

Many of the resources that I have found, unfortunately, encourage me to consider the lie as an untruth about myself: I am not lovable, I am not good enough, or I do not have what it takes. They say that these are the root lies, but they are not. These are merely surface lies that act as feeder roots, nourishing and sustaining the ugly lie underneath. This root lie has nothing to do with me and how lovable, good, or capable I am. It is much deeper. The lies of my fears have a bigger, "badder" lie underneath them all, and it has nothing to do with what I believe about myself. It is not a lie about who I am or what I can do. The lie underneath is a lie about God. It is a lie about who He is and what He can do.

This lie affects how we think, feel, and behave. This terrible lie about God does not allow us to live the kind of life that testifies to the greatness of God. Instead, our lives advertise that God is not good. Our anxiousness displays to all that God does not love me. God is not love. Our worry proclaims to everyone that God is not in control. Our lives publicize that God is not trustworthy. We must stop! We cannot continue spreading these lies about God. We need to recognize that the lie underneath is entirely about God. The lie underneath is attacking His attributes, His nature, His character, who He is. The lie is all about how loving, good, and capable God is.

Our Root Lies are Blasphemy

The foundation of my whole belief system is my theology of God; therefore, what I believe about Him will show in the way that I live. As A. W. Tozer recognized in his famous work, T*he Knowledge of the Holy*, the most significant fact about any man "is not what he at a given time may say or do, but what he in his deep heart conceives God to be like."[3] In our deep heart, aka the deep roots of our belief system, we answer who God is and what God is like. The Bible tells us God is good, loving, merciful, gracious, and faithful. The gospel message that Jesus Christ died for my sins, conquered death, and is coming again is fundamental to my beliefs. But have I somehow distorted my view of the gospel so that now I am believing lies—root lies that defame God's character? These lies that tell me I must work to gain God's approval; He doesn't really love me; I have to earn it (Ephesians 2:8–9). These lies that tell me that I need something else besides God to be fulfilled. He isn't enough (Psalm 34:10). Lies advise me that I deserve a healthy, happy life with no troubles. If God loved me, He would make life easy (Mark 8:34). Lies instruct me to follow my heart, telling me that God does not know what's best for me, but I do (Jeremiah 17:9). All these lies lead me away from the gospel message and the truth about God's character. These root lies are causing us to fear, and they are affecting our thoughts and feelings, leading us to behave in ways that continue to reinforce the lies. We need to realize that these anxious, negative thoughts that we allow ourselves to contemplate are based on root lies that we believe about the character of God. Our root lies are those thoughts that we would never speak out loud. Our root lies are blasphemy.

Underneath our fears and negative thoughts, down deep at the bottom, is our root lie about God. To discover what that lie is, we will have to begin excavation at the top, with a berry. Let me introduce you to what I call the Berry Bush. This bush is full of poisonous berries that represent barriers between God and us. These berries are those fears we continue to struggle with and those thoughts that stubbornly refuse to leave us alone. To eliminate these berries, we can't just pick them off; that won't work because they keep growing back. We will have to work hard to break up the soil, burrow down deep, and dig until we uncover the lie about God that is underneath. We will excavate it, pulling out the root, recognizing the harm it has caused us and those around us. Then we will plant a Truth Tree with a beautiful root that proclaims God's goodness, trustworthiness, and love.

I Do Believe! Help Me Overcome My Unbelief

All of us have lies deep within us that keep us from unashamedly jumping into Jesus's arms and living a life of complete faith in His provision, His acceptance, His plan, His goodness, and His love. I was reading in Mark chapter 9, when I saw myself in the father who brought his demon-possessed son to Jesus, asking Him to heal his son, saying, "*But if you can do anything, take pity on us and help us.*" "'*If you can'?" said Jesus. "Everything is possible for one who believes." Immediately, the boy's father exclaimed, "I do believe; help me overcome my unbelief!*" (Mark 9:22–24). That is precisely how I feel! I relate to this father's weakness in wanting to believe, but still feel unable to trust completely. This boy's father boldly exclaimed, "*I do believe!*" but then immediately confessed that he needs help with his unbelief. We are exactly the same. We say, "We believe," but we need to ask for help with our unbelief.

Many years ago, my parents gave me a hymnal devotional[4] for Christmas, and recently, rummaging through a closet looking for something else, I found it in a box full of old memories. I decided to put it out on my nightstand to read through again because I love hymns and the stories of how the hymn came to be, how God impressed these particular words upon each writer's heart. I'm often challenged by their faith and perseverance. This morning, I turned to "Tis So Sweet to Trust in Jesus." I have sung that song a thousand times, but as I sang it today, the last line of the chorus really struck me: "O for grace to trust Him more." Even though He has proved Himself over and over to me, I still need grace to trust Him more.

> 'Tis so sweet to trust in Jesus. Just to take Him at His word,
> Just to rest upon His promise. Just to know, "Thus saith the Lord"

Jesus, Jesus, how I trust Him. How I've proved Him o'er and o'er
Jesus, Jesus, precious Jesus. O for grace to trust Him more.[5]

This hymn was penned by Louisa Stead. One day, she, her husband, and four-year-old daughter Lilly were at the beach for a picnic when they heard a young boy crying out for help. Her husband rushed to him in the water, but Louisa and Lilly watched helplessly as both Mr. Stead and the boy drowned. After his death, getting by became extremely difficult for Louisa and her daughter. Poverty struck, and they were in dire need. One morning, she woke to find food and money on her doorstep. That same day, she sat down and wrote this hymn.[6] The lyrics are simple to say, but they are not random rhymes. Stead knew the faithfulness of God. She was certain that He was always with her, true to His promises and offering her rest, joy, and peace. There is nothing superficial in her words. Tragedy had taught her to trust, and through it all, she chose to describe trusting in Jesus as "sweet." Stead's testimony displays a different way of responding to unfathomable loss by trusting in Jesus and asking for grace to trust Him more.

This reminds me of another hymn that shares that same sentiment, "It is Well with My Soul" by Horatio Spafford. When the ship sank, and his four daughters drowned on the way to England, he chose to say, "When sorrows like sea billows roll . . . it is well, it is well with my soul."[7] To be able to write these words after such a personal tragedy amazes me. When loss hits us, and our equilibrium is struck, lies softly sweep in. Blaming God seems the most plausible answer to our pain. When we feel the loss of our own sense of control, lies begin to make sense to us. We clamor for God to bend to our will.

In Mark 9, as the desperate father looks on his son rolling on the ground, convulsing, and foaming at the mouth, he pleads with Jesus to accept whatever small faith he has, alongside his doubt and fear. Jesus welcomes the father's genuine heart, both his boldness and limitations. This father's attitude of trust is not something that he could conjure up on his own. He needed help, help with his unbelief. He knew he couldn't just dig deeper within himself or pull up his bootstraps and have the necessary faith. He was overwhelmed, despairing, anxious, and willing to admit that he did not believe. We are like him. We want to be self-sufficient and find it inside of us, but faith is a gift from God, who is the author and perfecter of our faith. He knows that we will not find it within ourselves but invites us to find it within Him. Don't beat yourself up for not having enough faith. Instead, ask our generous God who delights in providing what we need. "O for grace to trust Him more," I repeat that last line over and over. It is exactly what my heart cries out. Lord, I want to trust You more and stop believing lies! Give me the grace to trust You more, to recognize these lies, and to discern how they are affecting me.

Listening for Truth

1. Is it possible to not listen to the lies of our fears?
2. What has your journey to stop believing lies been like?
3. Think of a time when you cried out to Jesus, "Help my unbelief!" How did He answer?
4. Where do you need to ask God for grace to trust Him more?

Chapter 2

HOW THE LIE UNDERNEATH IS AFFECTING MY THOUGHTS, FEELINGS, AND BEHAVIOR

I was in the kitchen washing dishes when my husband, Paul, came to me with a worried expression. He shoved his phone in my face and said, "Look what Bob wrote!" I asked, "Is this Bob our ministry partner?" The text read, "We need to talk. Call me when you have a moment." My stomach dropped. "What could he want? Why does he want to talk? Paul, do you know?" I asked. I could see the rush of anxiety on Paul's face, and I felt it too.

Until I read that text, I had been singing along with the radio and happily going about my business, but suddenly, I stood paralyzed with fear. This all happened in an instant. I went from peaceful to a full-fledged storm of emotions. How? My beliefs were affecting my thoughts, and my thoughts were controlling my emotions and actions.

Here I stood clutching a cell phone, anticipating the worst possible scenario, and plotting what to do next. My husband and I were so worried because our finances were a mess. We work for a ministry where we raise money to support our family. We have lots of families and churches who give monthly to be on our team of ministry partners who provide for us so that we can be in full-time ministry. Our account had suffered some hits lately, and it seemed like another one was coming. Now, seeing this text, we expected Bob to share with us that he was leaving our ministry partner team.

What Am I Believing?

For a long while now, God has been teaching me to trust that He will provide for me. I know all the verses that remind us to be strong and not to worry because God is caring for us, but living that out is not always easy. It's one thing to memorize a verse and be able to recite it, but simply knowing it by heart doesn't mean I'm truly practicing it in my daily life. Jesus says, "*Do not be anxious about your life*" (Matthew 6:25 ESV), and in Philippians, Paul instructs us, "*Do not be anxious about anything*" (Philippians 4:6). Although I know these verses, I must not genuinely believe them because if I did, my thoughts would be different. How I feel and how I behave would be different. So, I began to ask myself, what am I believing?

The phone rang. It was Bob. I took a deep breath, trying to remember what Paul and I had rehearsed, how we would answer, and respond. Out of my mouth came a weak greeting. The cordial question of "How are you doing?" brought forth a sarcastic, ugly response in my mind, but thankfully, Paul answered for us. It took a few moments, but soon I realized . . . wait. This is not at all what I expected. He is actually saying he wants to increase his giving! As the conversation went on, I could hear the gentle whispers of the Holy Spirit reminding me that He has me in His hand. He will provide for me. He loves me. We hung up the phone and got on our knees, repenting (once again) of our unbelief and worshiping Him for His lavish love. I could barely utter, "God, why do I continue to doubt you? You tell me in Your Word over and over that You will take care of me, that You will provide for me. You show me time and time again that You love me, but still, I do not truly believe You."

Our Thoughts, Emotions, and Behavior

My thoughts affect how I act. My thoughts were filled with worry and fret over finances. I behaved as if I were someone who had never heard the words of Jesus, promising me that as He watches over the sparrows, how much more will He care for me. In fact, He has the hairs of my head numbered and reminds me time and again not to be afraid (Matthew 10:29–31). I don't know if you can relate, but I think you can. I think that probably you are a lot like me. You know all the Bible verses. You have stood up and publicly shared with others about God's faithfulness in your life. But then something happens, and you forget. You say that you believe, but your thoughts, emotions, and behavior do not agree. Your thoughts, emotions, and behavior do not testify of God's faithfulness.

Our thoughts impact how we feel, and those feelings influence how we act. Our emotions and behaviors will reinforce what we think. Before you know it, we are going in circles and have gotten ourselves in a real repetitive cycle because our emotions and behavior reinforce our thinking patterns. This cycle is a key focus area of a mental health treatment approach called Cognitive Behavioral

Therapy, which is discussed in *The Lies We Believe* by Chris Thurman.[1] It is a practical method of psychotherapy that helps with anxiety. It purports that the way we think affects our mood, which in turn affects our behavior, and these three reinforce our beliefs, which start the cycle all over again. By identifying and challenging our core beliefs, we can interrupt the cycle. This is the repeated pattern that our thoughts follow:[2]

My thoughts	Affect →	How I feel
How I feel	Influences →	My behavior
My behavior	Reinforces →	What I believe
What I believe	Impacts →	My thoughts

Ruts

Have you ever gotten your car stuck in the mud? I grew up in a small town in Texas in the country where the dirt roads can develop some deep ruts after a good rain. My family lived in a doublewide trailer about a mile off the main road on a typical dirt road. It was often full of ruts. I remember as a new teenage driver trying so hard to stay out of them, but ultimately falling in with a thud, cursed to follow along the way of the furrowed groove with no option of escape for several stretches of road (even when I needed to turn left to get to my friend's house). When I think about those ruts, I think about my thought cycle and how the more I consider a lie and reinforce it through my actions, the deeper the rut I am making. As I ruminate over that lie, allowing it to affect my feelings and behaving as if I believe it, eventually I do. That is why I act like I don't believe that God will take care of me the way that He takes care of the sparrows. Because I created the lie, I let it lead my thoughts down into a deep, furrowed groove that carries me along and reinforces my wrong beliefs. From then on, whenever that thought comes into my head, it will continue to broaden the expanse of the rut, making it wider and deeper each time.

In my childhood, I remember looking out my bedroom window after the rain had stopped. The sun emerged. The dirt road was just slightly damp, slowly hardening as the sunrays stiffened the soil. In the distance, the sound of a deep diesel engine rumbled. A pickup truck with a grader attached to the back of it appeared on our dirt road. Behind it, the truck dragged a wide, heavy grader that smoothed out the ruts. Back and forth it would drive down our road, making several passes to ensure that they were gone and that the road was level again. I was grateful because I would not fall into those tracks again, and I could easily turn left and drive to my friend's house without any trouble. Those ruts are such a visual depiction of how my thoughts can get me stuck. The more I ruminate on a berry thought, the bigger the gap. My thoughts careen into the crevice with a thud, cursed to stay in that groove and follow along the way of the rut with my mind, body, and mood pulled toward the deeper part of it. This is more than just a groove affecting my thoughts and feelings; it impacts my beliefs, causing me to contradict myself and not live in the peace that Jesus says He has given me (John 14:27). However, there is more to this illustration because here come those trucks dragging graders behind them to eliminate the ruts! This book will show you a way to bring the pickup trucks with the graders to your mind and level out the furrowed grooves that are full of poisonous berries.

OK, obviously, I am not a neuroscientist, and this illustration can only go so far because our neural pathways are more complex than ruts in a road, but it has helped me to realize that my thoughts are not just benign ideas that flit and float in and out of my brain. They do affect everything—my mind, attitude, and comportment. Those thoughts that I ruminate on will not only affect my mood and conduct, but ultimately what I believe, by creating an easy path for my thoughts to continue down each time. Neurosurgeon Dr. Lee Warren explains that "when you think about something enough times from a particular point of view, you create ruts and synapses in your brain that automate those thoughts and make it easier for them to perpetuate."[3] He points out that every day we have thousands of automatic thoughts, of which many are not true. When we repeatedly have negative thoughts and behaviors, we create a neural pathway in our brain, and each time it makes it easier for our mind to go that way, creating a rut and ultimately reinforcing the lie. We are stuck in the cycle of fearful thoughts, burdened feelings, and agitated behavior.

Once we understand this thought cycle and its impact, we will recognize that our thoughts really do affect everything. It is time that we seriously consider what we allow ourselves to reflect on. Because those ideas that roll around in our head don't ask for permission to stay, they simply continue rolling around, impacting us. They will have a say in how we feel, and those emotions will influence our behavior. Unfortunately, we will continue in this cycle with those same fears occupying our thought life, influencing our emotions, and affecting our behavior. These are the poisonous berries growing on your Berry Bush. These poisonous berries are affecting everything! How did we get into this predicament? What started this vicious thought cycle? Let's go back to the beginning and learn, as Eve did, that it all begins with a lie about God.

Listening for Truth

1. Consider any disparity between what you know in your heart and what your thoughts, emotions, and behavior show. If someone could eavesdrop on your thoughts, what would they hear?
2. Think about an experience where you behaved as if you had never heard of Jesus's care for the sparrows and for you. What were you thinking and feeling?
3. Look back at the image of the thought cycle and consider how your thoughts are affecting your feelings and behavior. What kind of thoughts seem to be recurring and affecting you the most?
4. Name a thought that is creating a rut in your mind. Now imagine a truck and grader coming to level out that rut.

Chapter 3

THE ORIGIN OF OUR LIE UNDERNEATH

After that worrisome text and phone call, I asked myself, "What am I believing?" It became apparent to me by my actions and emotions that I was believing a lie about God. I was stuck in the thought cycle. That realization drove me to try to figure out how to stop believing and living out the lie. It is the basis of this book: How can we recognize the lies we believe, see how they are changing our hearts, our feelings, and how those lies are affecting our actions? To be able to do that, first, we will have to go back to the very beginning with the first lie that Satan told Eve.

> *Now the serpent who was the most cunning of all the wild animals that the Lord God had made. He said to the woman, "Did God really say "'You can't eat from any tree in the garden?'" The woman said to the serpent, "We may eat the fruit from the trees in the garden. But about the fruit of the tree in the middle of the garden, God said, 'You must not eat it or touch it, or you will die.'"*

"No! You will not die," the serpent said to the woman. "In fact, God knows that when you eat it your eyes will be opened and you will be like God, knowing good and evil." Then the woman saw that the tree was good for food and delightful to look at, and that it was desirable for obtaining wisdom. So she took some of its fruit and ate it; she also gave some to her husband, who was with her, and he ate it.

—Genesis 3:1–6 HCSB

When Satan approached Eve, he asked her a question. "*Did God really say . . . ?*" With his incredulous tone, he planted seeds of skepticism in Eve's mind. The suggestion that she should question God's integrity was presented. It made God seem ungenerous and insincere, causing Eve to focus on the one thing that God had forbidden. Had God really wanted to keep something from her? Was He denying her something pleasurable? Maybe God wasn't truly good, and maybe He really didn't love her or want what was best for her. Why would He put restrictions on her? Didn't He want her to be happy?

This line of thinking reminds me of what I have heard from my children when they wanted something that I knew wasn't good for them. I know you are probably thinking that I am talking about candy. Almost every trip to the grocery store has included some form of this thinking being visibly displayed. However, right now our household is working through our child's desire for a smartphone. Why are we keeping something so good from our own child? Why would we deny them the pleasure of the apps they want? Maybe we are not good parents. Maybe we don't love our children. Perhaps we don't want what is best for them. Why would we put restrictions on when they can use their phone? Don't we want them to be happy? Of course, it is easy for us to see in our children's behavior, but can we see it in our own thinking? Are we just as guilty of accusing God of keeping something from us?

With Satan's suggestion to Eve that God is not good, he created doubt about God's character and caused her to question God's motives. He didn't stop there; he came right out and called God a liar when he said, "*No! You will not die.*" Here, Eve should have stopped him, realizing the obvious complete contradiction to what God had said. Instead, Eve took in the lie. She considered his words, dwelling on them and allowing them to persuade her to engage her feelings. He played on Eve's desire for control. In effect, he is saying, "If you do eat, you will see things the way that God sees them. Your eyes will be opened." This was a partial truth. If Eve had only known the deception of what her eyes would be open to, the misery this decision would bring! She was hoping to be like God, deciding what was right for herself, but she will find out that her eyes will be opened to the reality that she is naked and ashamed.

The chance to judge for herself what was good or bad was just enough to pull Eve in and motivate her to consider it. "You will be like God. God is holding out on you, and you don't even know it. God is not good, not really. If He were good, He would give you everything that you want. If God were good, you would have everything that He has." Satan offered her a chance to be just like God, having the ability to make her own decisions about what was right and wrong without God defining it for her.

Dissatisfaction began to brew in her heart as Eve entertained the thoughts that had been planted. She considered the serpent's slander. As she ruminated, she acknowledged the possibility that God was perhaps not entirely truthful with her. Those thoughts brought the feeling of discontent and led to anger and jealousy. Why would God hold out on her? Her emotions told her to take the fruit. Eve used her feelings to justify her wrong actions. Do you see how her thoughts led to her feelings of discontent, which then rationalized her behavior?

Reader, I would prefer not to share this story with you, but I feel compelled to give you an illustration of this in my own life. This is an example of how I, like Eve, allowed my thoughts, which were based on a lie about God, to affect my feelings. And that brought dissatisfaction that I then used to justify my bad behavior. As a mother, I hold high expectations for harmony within the family. I do not like sibling squabbles and have tried very hard to instill within our family Ephesians 5:2, "*Live a life filled with love*" (NLT). That expectation is why, on one beautiful evening while on a vacation in Colorado, I blew it. We had gone out to eat and for ice cream. It should have been a fun family evening. On the drive downtown, the boys began to pick on each other. Throughout dinner, there was kicking under the table and shoving in our booth. Each time, my husband and I tried to remind them of the Golden Rule and help them to be kind toward each other.

As we walked to the ice cream parlor, I heard them calling each other mean names, and I gave in to the thoughts that had been ruminating in my mind, "You are a bad mother. You should know how to help your children get along and love each other. You don't know what you are doing. You are wrecking their lives and yours." With the ice cream still dripping down our cones, the boys gave each other a few more forceful pushes, and that was it for me. I lost it! Right in the middle of all the happy vacationers waiting in line to enter and order their delicious treats, I began to go berserk. I couldn't hold back my aggravation. Yes, I was frustrated at their behavior, but my thoughts had been telling me all night that I was a failure as a mother. Now it was apparent to all. I took off. I left the kids standing there with my husband and walked away as fast as I could. My family tried to catch up with me, the kids crying and apologizing, but I wouldn't listen. I couldn't hear. I was too far in my head with my disturbed rhetoric. I was justifying my anger and outburst. I felt like my screaming at them was warranted. Actually, it was all I knew how to do because a lie was dictating my feelings. My lie seemed to be all about me being a bad mom, but it was really all about God. Just like Eve's lie, my lie got me to the place where I was ready to rationalize my decision to throw a fit. The root lie was about God's character. I was listening to the lie, making it about me. Still, as I asked myself why I thought that, I began to uncover the reasons: I don't know what I'm doing, I don't have what it takes to be their mother, I don't believe that God will be all I need, I don't trust that He has equipped me, I feel like He is holding out on me, and ultimately I believe that God is not good. My root lie is the same as Eve's. God is not good. I had allowed that lie to affect my feelings, bringing me to a moment of such dissatisfaction that I reacted in a big way and then validated my actions with that lie. It is a predictable pattern. Eve fell for it, and so did I.

This destructive cycle continues in us today. We all buy into this lie, but we don't realize it because our lips are proclaiming that God is good. We speak the truth, but when things don't work out like we hoped, when healing doesn't come, when we suffer loss, when tragedy hits us, when we pray and God answers no . . . at that moment our heart begins to question God's character and think, "Why would You keep this from me?"

Eve looked at the fruit. She saw that "*the tree was good for food.*" She dismissed the fact that God did not call it good for her. It appealed to her appetite. It would satisfy her physical needs. It was "*delightful to look at.*" As Eve took in its beauty, she yearned to taste it. Jesus called our eyes the lamp to our body (Matthew 6:22). What we look intently upon will become our intent. Her pride and desire for self-sufficiency arose within her as she held the fruit and believed the serpent's claim that it was "*desirable for obtaining wisdom.*" She made the deliberate choice to go against God's command and ate the fruit.

Self

Eve had been convinced that she would be enlightened, but from the moment she took her first bite of the fruit, her life changed. Before everything in her life was right, nothing was wrong. She literally lived in paradise, where intimacy with God was the center of her life. She didn't need to cover herself, nor had she ever known a reason to hide. Eve had never experienced shame or fear. When the serpent approached Eve and invited her to entertain thoughts questioning God's goodness and God's love, the temptation was more than simply eating a piece of fruit; it was a coup, a revolt, a seizure of power. Before she took and ate of the fruit, her creator God was the center of everything. She and her husband, Adam, were made in His image and cherished Him. When they awoke, their first thought was Him. They delighted in Him. They enjoyed an intimate relationship with God, living in complete innocence and trust, but not now. Although God had been the center of their life, self had taken that spot now. When the Lord approached Adam and Eve after they had been hiding from Him, He gave them the opportunity to confess, but all they did was blame each other, the serpent, and even God to protect self. When God asked them, "*Who told you that you were naked?*" the answer was self. They were now self-aware, self-serving, self-conscious, and self-focused. God was no longer the center of their lives. They had broken their trust with God and, in doing so, Timothy Jennings explains, they had lost their "innate sense of safety and security. Their experience of peace gone, they became consumed with fear and guilt, which led to a drive for self-preservation."[1] Their focal point had been switched to self. Now, self dominates our every thought, feeling, and behavior. Self is what drives our lives and torments us with fears. It leads us to doubt God's goodness, love, and trustworthiness.

Your Life Is Shaped By Your Thoughts

When we, like Eve, begin to doubt God's goodness, we demonstrate that we too have been ensnared. All of mankind has been caught up in believing lies about God's character. No one has escaped the effect of lies on our lives. We are all susceptible to the devil's schemes. He continues to use deception in our thoughts to confuse us and blind us to the truth. This is where our Berry Bush flourishes, and the berries are abundant.

Nancy DeMoss Wolgemuth, in her book *Lies Women Believe and the Truths that Set Them Free*, points out that "we listen to the lie; we dwell on it until we believe it; finally, we act on it."[2] Like Eve, we make the decision to give Satan our ear. As we give attention to those thoughts, at first it doesn't seem like a big deal to mull them over, so we allow ourselves to dwell on the thoughts. That lie begins to influence our feelings, impacting our behavior. Ultimately, we begin to believe it. When that thought shows up again, we allow it, and the next time we do it again, and then again, creating a "groove" in our hearts. Wolgemuth calls this a "sinful stronghold"[3] The Bible uses the military image of a stronghold, painting in our minds the picture of a well-fortified building high atop a mountain. In ancient times, it was the most defensible against attack. In 2 Corinthians 10, the Apostle Paul compared that type of stronghold to the stronghold in our minds.

> *For though we live in the world, we do not wage war as the world does. The weapons we fight with are not the weapons of the world. On the contrary, they have divine power to demolish strongholds. We demolish arguments and every pretension that sets itself up against the knowledge of God, and we take captive every thought to make it obedient to Christ.*
>
> —2 Corinthians 10:3–5

In his book, *Every Thought Captive*, pastor Kyle Idleman defines a stronghold as "a lie we believe and live by. Strongholds are formed by ingrained patterns of thinking that are opposed to God's truth and wisdom."[4] These self-exalting thoughts are dense barriers that keep our hearts from God. The deceptive thoughts, arrogant attitudes, and contradictions of God's word become reinforced, creating mental fortresses and "until we take them captive, they will hold us captive."[5]

Tonight, a friend came over for dinner. We started talking about lies and how hard it is to stop believing them. He was excited about a new study that his community group at church had been going through together. The study is based on a book about discipleship called *A Deeper Walk,*[6] by Marcus Warner, in which he explains that many Christians remain stuck in strongholds, living as victims, despite the fact that freedom is intended to be a vital part of following Christ. As we stood in the kitchen over the barbecue buffet line, my friend explained that Warner's book shows how lies creep in and take hold of us. His eyes were full of the kind of excitement you feel when you know and have experienced what you are talking about. With resounding conviction, my friend shared, "It all begins with a wounded part of my heart that opens me up to a lie from the devil and keeps me from trusting God." He went on to describe how that lie causes him to make a vow about how he has to take control because he can't trust God with his pain. Vows like, "I will never let this happen again" produce strongholds that "create a sense of hopelessness."[7] Bit by bit, this stronghold will become a part of our belief system, and we may not even realize that a piece of our heart has been taken over by a lie about God. That lie will feel so true. We will walk around in complete ignorance, continuing to blame our situation, accuse others, attribute it all to our lack of self-control, and remain unaware that the root of our thoughts is a lie about God.

Proverbs 4:23 warns us, "*Be careful how you think; your life is shaped by your thoughts*" (GNT). We must guard our hearts with more vigilance than anything else and carefully watch over what we think about because everything we do comes from our thoughts. Our thoughts will find their way into our hearts and affect how we feel. Our thoughts will validate how we act and eventually reinforce a wrong belief. This dangerous cycle of wrong thoughts, emotions, behaviors, and beliefs will continue until we do something about it. If we allow ourselves to persist in this behavior and thought cycle and do not consider how to intentionally attempt to change, then we will simply recreate the same behaviors and thought patterns. We will be living our lives based on a lie, but not just any lie, a lie about God.

The inception of all our fears can be traced back to the Garden of Eden. Here we find that Satan's attack on the sovereignty of God and His character is the origin of our struggle with fear and anxiety. All the berries on our Berry Bush can be traced back to a lie about who God is. What we think about God or what we don't think about God will dictate our fears. That is why Satan is after our thoughts.

Listening for Truth

1. How might you be falling for these same lies that Eve allowed the serpent to plant in her mind? (God is holding out on me, God is not truly good, God doesn't love me, God is not in control, God won't give me all that I need, I can't trust God.)
2. What we look intently upon will become our intent. Consider Eve's experience with the fruit and compare it to something you look intently upon. Then read James 1:25. Ask yourself what you are looking intently upon. How is focusing on that thing influencing you?
3. Think about a time when you, like Eve, used your feelings to justify your actions.
4. Knowing that the origin of our struggle with fear and anxiety is a lie about God's character, how will that impact the way you view the fear and anxiety that manifests in your daily life?

PART II

SATAN IS AFTER YOUR THOUGHTS

Chapter 4

WARNING! DANGEROUS DECEIVER AHEAD!

If you're like me, you're busy living your life and not considering what your thoughts are focused on, but the devil is. He is utterly obsessed with what you and I are thinking about because he knows that our thoughts lead to our feelings, which in turn affect our behavior and shape what we believe, especially what we believe about God. Satan is after our thoughts. We are traveling down life's highway, and along the way, we see a guy in a bright neon reflective vest wearing a hard hat. He looks familiar. Could that be? Yes, it is. It's Jesus! He is holding up warning signs that read, "Danger! Deceiver Ahead," "Keep Right—Roaring Lion Ahead," "Disguised Angel of Light Coming Up," "Keep Right, Liar in Left Lane," "Be Prepared for Thief Coming to Steal, Kill and Destroy." He is warning us of Satan's schemes, cautioning us that Satan is after our thoughts. Are we too caught up gazing at our own reflection in the rear-view mirror, or are we so distracted that we have taken our attention off the road? Will we notice the blinking lights and big orange triangles alerting us that there is a big fat liar on the road planning our demise and licking his chops, waiting for any opportunity to contrive lies about God's character?

When we lived in Madrid, Spain, we had been warned of pickpockets. We understood that we should expect them anytime we went downtown, and we were to be prepared. One afternoon, I was on the subway herding our young kids onto the escalator. Because of the risk, I knew better than to wear my backpack on my back. However, it was hard to carry the baby wearing the backpack in front, so I switched it to my back and picked up the baby. As we rode up the escalator, I heard a funny noise. It sounded like a faint jingle of keys. I turned and saw my keys attached to my wallet in the hand of a girl behind me. Busted! I stuck my hand out, palm up; she placed my wallet in it and ran away. I was so glad to get it back and thankful that I had attached the keys to the wallet, but I was kicking myself for making it so easy for the pickpocket to get to it. She was good at thieving. I would not have known at all that she had unzipped my pack and stuck her hand in my bag while I was wearing it, if it had not been for the jingle of my keys. She was slick and had it down to an art form. I knew there were thieves just waiting for someone as distracted and available as me. Just as I was warned when we moved to Europe to beware of pickpockets, the Bible warns us of the evil one who is after us, who is so crafty that he is nearly undetectable.

Satan is always whispering lies in our ears, trying to deceive us. He wants us to believe that God is not good. He whispers, "God doesn't love me," hoping you'll repeat it to yourself. "God doesn't care about me. God is not trustworthy. God is not enough. God is too restrictive. God won't forgive me." He is doing everything he can to tempt us to doubt God's character. Our enemy is the one cultivating those berries on our Berry Bush. The lies that he used on Eve remain in his arsenal. Even today, we are still vulnerable to his lies about God.

In John 8:44, Jesus describes the devil as "*a murderer from the beginning. He has always hated the truth, because there is no truth in him. When he lies, it is consistent with his character; for he is a liar and the father of lies*" (NLT). Satan specifically wants to destroy God's reputation and concentrates his efforts on those of us who follow Christ. That is why we must not remain ignorant and unaware. He is after our thoughts! Satan has predictable tactics and uses the same tricks over and over to make us oblivious, proud, isolated, selfish, discouraged, and anxious.[1] Peter warns us, "*Stay alert! Watch out for your great enemy, the devil. He prowls around like a roaring lion, looking for someone to devour. Stand firm against him and be strong in your faith*" (1 Peter 5:8–9 NLT). This is our reality: we have a great enemy who is stalking us, sedulously sneaking around, whispering in our ear, putting wrong ideas in our heads, ready and waiting to devour us. However, it is evident that this is not our perspective because we go about our day-to-day life without recognizing the impact of those negative thoughts. Through our negligence, we allow Satan to pounce on us, enter our minds, and plant seeds of doubt about who God is, all the while we don't even notice.

Scripture Warns Us About Him

We should take notice, because the Bible cautions us repeatedly to be on guard. Paul instructs the church in Ephesians 6 to "*Put on all the armor that God gives you, so that you will be able to stand up against the Devil's evil tricks*" (6:11 GNT). Our adversary is cunning, crafty, and calculating. He uses flaming arrows and snares. His goal is to destroy us. He is called the deceiver, the accuser, the murderer, and the father of lies. We need God's armor to stand against his scheming. Each piece of God's armor represents a part of Him and His strength that He provides to His children. In Ephesians, before Paul begins describing each piece of spiritual armor, he reminds the church to "*be strong in the Lord and in His mighty power*" (Ephesians 6:10). Only by means of the Lord's strength, solely by His mighty power, can you and I take our stand against the devil's evil tricks. Four times in Ephesians 6:11–14, we are told to "stand" (emphasis mine):

- Verse 11: "*Put on the full armor of God so that you can take your* ***stand*** *against the devil's schemes.*"
- Verse 13: "*Therefore put on the full armor of God, so that when the day of evil comes, you may be able to* ***stand*** *your ground, and after you have done everything, to* ***stand***."
- Verse 14: "***Stand*** *firm then.*"

Standing requires that you be awake.

Many years ago, when we had only two young children, we returned to the United States to raise support for a few months. A church graciously offered us an apartment to stay in while we were back. One night, around three in the morning, we were awakened by the blaring sound of the smoke alarm. I awoke, jumped out of bed, and ran to our kids' room to wake them. As I tried to rouse the old-est, I picked him up and set him on his feet. "Good, he is awake," I thought. Then I moved to wake up his baby brother. When I turned around, I expected to see my son ready to run down the stairs with me. Instead, he was curled on the floor, sound asleep despite the blaring alarm. I tried again in vain to get him to stand, but it was impossible. His legs were like jelly. I picked him up, grabbed his sleeping baby brother, and carried them both down the stairs. He didn't wake up until we got into the car. This image of his legs continuing to buckle as I tried to get him to stand reminds me that for us to take our stand against the devil's schemes, we must be awake and watchful.

We are told to stand, to resist movement, and not collapse under pressure, but to hold our position when we come against evil. We win this battle by standing firm even when we are afraid. Imagine what it was like for the Israelites as they escaped slavery in Egypt. Soon after they started into the desert, they were trapped, faced with the Red Sea in front of them and the Egyptian army closing in behind. In that moment, Moses called out, "*Do not be afraid.* ***Stand firm*** *and you will see the deliverance the Lord will bring you today*" (Exodus 14:13 emphasis mine). As His children, we stand in God's faithful protection. We stand, not in our own strength, but in His strength. We stand in faith, trusting in God's sovereign authority and power.

Another example of God telling his children to stand firm is in 2 Chronicles 20. A vast army was coming against Judah. King Jehoshaphat called for a nationwide fast. The people came together to seek the Lord, and Jehoshaphat prayed, "*We do not know what to do, but our eyes are on you*" (20:12). The Lord replied to them:

> *You will not have to fight this battle. Take up your positions; stand firm and see the deliverance the Lord will give you, Judah and Jerusalem. Do not be afraid; do not be discouraged. Go out to face them tomorrow, and the Lord will be with you.*
>
> —2 Chronicles 20:17

God would be with them, but they had to go out and face them. They had to stand firm. We are not facing a physical enemy army, but every day we are engaged in a spiritual battle taking place in our mind, fighting temptations, wrong thoughts, and lies. God tells us to stand firm, stand strong, be steadfast in our faith, and we will see His deliverance.

I like to take walks around my neighborhood, and so does our sweet, gentle dog, Lil' Bill. If we go out early enough, we don't see many other dogs, which is fine by me because I am afraid of aggressive dogs. The other day we rounded the corner and suddenly from behind a house, a vicious looking pit bull, baring its teeth, ran straight toward us. My heart stopped as Lil' Bill cowered behind me. What could we do? I panicked as the violent brute of a dog rushed forward! Suddenly and abruptly, the dog was jolted backward with a strong force. I realized then that he was chained to a tree. He had run the length of his chain but could not reach us on the sidewalk where we stood with our knees quaking. Had we gone a few feet inside his yard, closer to his reach, that dog would have devoured us. The devil is like a pit bull chained to a tree. He is intimidating, loud, and aggressive, but he is limited. His reach extends only as far as the chain allows. Because of Christ's victory on the cross, he is powerless to harm us. When we are standing firm, planted in the truth of who God is and who we are in Him, we learn to recognize the chain, step out of the devil's reach, and walk in the freedom Christ has already secured for us. Yet many of us live as though the chain does not exist, living as though fear was in charge. Strongholds form when we linger too close—when we repeatedly listen to that devil dog's growls and agree with his lies. That is when he pounces, and his lies begin to make sense to us; those thoughts infect us with fear and worry. The berries on our bush get bigger, and their lie about who God is roots down deeper, fortifying itself with more and more false feeder roots. The deceiver's schemes will have worked if we do not heed God's warnings and stand firm against Satan.

Listening for Truth

1. What is on the warning sign that Jesus is holding up to show you?
2. Why do you think that we, as followers of Jesus, do not take these warnings more seriously?
3. What does "standing firm" look like for you?
4. Can you recognize a lie about God's character the devil is whispering into your thoughts and how it's creating a berry on your Berry Bush?

Chapter 5

HOW TO STAND AGAINST SATAN

In Ephesians, the apostle Paul reminds us that "*our struggle is not against flesh and blood, but against the rulers, against the authorities, against the powers of this dark world and against the spiritual forces of evil in the heavenly realms*" (Ephesians 6:12). Our struggle is not against other humans. The fight is spiritual, not physical. Unfortunately, we don't understand this reality, and instead of fighting our actual opponent, we choose to see other humans as our enemy. Too often, when we come into conflict or have difficulties with another person, we forget entirely who is actually working against us. When we are so angry with others, do we realize that they are just as much of a target as we are? They have a bull's-eye on their backs just as we do. Jesus tells us to pray for those who persecute us. He calls us to love our enemies. He wants us to have a perspective full of compassion, not condemnation, and to see each other not as adversaries, but as brothers and sisters. Because the real object of our anger is not another human, but the forces of evil who seek our ruin.

To win this battle, we need to fight the right opponent. We know what physical combat looks like, but how does one confront a spiritual battle? The opponent is invisible. We can't see what we are fighting against. This warfare manifests as an internal struggle, deep within our thoughts, where we experience anxiety, fear, doubt, guilt, and despair. Often, this spiritual wrestling begins when we find ourselves in situations that challenge our beliefs. All our spiritual battles come down to this: Will we stand firm in the truth of who God is, or will we believe lies about Him? To be equipped for this type of fighting—this kind of unseen, inner, spiritual battle, Paul tells us to put on all of God's armor. His armor will protect us with His truth, righteousness, peace, faith, salvation, and Word. Paul begins his description of God's armor with the truth.

Belt of Truth

"Mom!" my youngest son ran to me excitedly. He had just returned home from a school retreat. "You've got to see this video. Look how high in the air I am! See how I'm not holding onto anything, and I'm way up in the air, walking across a log. It was so hard, but I did it!" He explained how he and his sixth-grade class had participated in a ropes course. As we watched videos of his daring feats, he shared how scared he was being so high up with nothing to hold onto, but because of the harness he was wearing, he felt protected. The harness, he explained, was a kind of belt that he wore around his legs and waist that attached him to a safety line. When I asked him how he was able to convince himself to do such a daring feat, he answered confidently, "Even though what I was doing was dangerous, I knew that the belt anchored me and was keeping me secure. Just knowing that the belt was giving me some stability made it possible for me to keep going."

"*Stand firm then, with the belt of truth buckled around your waist*" (Ephesians 6:14). When we symbolically fasten the belt of truth, we secure ourselves in the stability that Christ provides. A Roman soldier put on this belt first because other pieces of armor, like the breastplate and the sword, were attached to it. The belt holds everything together. This belt is wide, covers much of the soldier's torso, and provides essential support. Truth is our support and upholds everything. It is our foundation, giving us security and steadiness as we stand. God's truth is absolute. His truth imbues who and whose I am. Isaiah described the future Messiah saying, "*He will wear righteousness like a belt and truth like an undergarment*" (Isaiah 11:5 NLT). Just as the belt secures our armor, the truth about God's character stabilizes us. Jesus is the revelation of God's character, and He calls Himself the truth (John 14:6). Righteousness and faithfulness are the foundation of who He is. His truth reminds me of what is real, no matter what my berries are telling me. Satan is all about obstructing, distracting, and causing us to stumble. He aims to deceive us by shading reality, causing temporal things to appear especially valuable to us, and seducing us away from what we know is true. When we inspect our berries, we will find that they are not based in the truth of God's character. To fight this spiritual battle, we must have God's truth wrapped around us, instead of our anxious thoughts.

Breastplate of Righteousness

Paul's instructions are to "*stand, therefore, with . . . righteousness like armor on your chest*" (Ephesians 6:14 HCSB). You and I have no righteousness in us, nothing that will protect us from our enemy, but when we give our lives to Jesus, making Him our Lord and Savior, His righteousness becomes ours.

School was about to begin, and our oldest child gleefully gathered all his supplies together in the dining room. Scattered all over the table were crayons, construction paper, markers, glue, scissors, and more. As we looked through the school's checklist to be certain we had everything he needed for his first day, we noticed an asterisk reminding us to make sure that we had labeled everything with his name. He wanted to do it, so He got out a sharpie and marked his lunchbox, water bottle, and other assorted school supplies. When he picked up his school uniform jacket, he asked me, "Where should I write my name? Where is the best place?" I looked for a tag in the back and then noticed a large label that read, "This jacket belongs to ______." I told my son, "This blank here is where you should write your name because it shows that it belongs to you."

Just like my son's school uniform jacket, our breastplate has a label. It reads, "This righteousness belongs to Jesus." Although we are the ones wearing it, it is not ours, and yet we are covered and defined by it. Our heart is protected and sealed by His finished work, not because of our efforts or achievements. His righteousness protects our heart in such a way that we surrender to His ways even when we are faced with grief and pain. The protection that His righteousness provides strengthens our hearts, enabling us to renounce selfishness, choose forgiveness, and live a life that honors God. We put on the breastplate by pursuing God's kingdom, trusting in His righteousness, and allowing Him to rule our lives. We know we are wearing His breastplate when God reveals a part of us that we need to confess and repent, and we choose to obey and accept His remolding and reshaping of our hearts. However, if we do not listen, we loosen our armor. When that happens, it opens up a section just big enough to allow the enemy's arrows in. Our thoughts will lead us to rely on our own righteousness. Our lies will harden our hearts, causing us to excuse sin in our lives. We will refuse to forgive, waiting for the other person to apologize first. Although we won't notice the shift, our perspective will have moved to worldly things. We are no longer wearing the breastplate of righteousness. Our Berry Bush has grown and is multiplying. Its roots are burrowing down deep into our belief system. Lies about God's character are becoming stronger and growing more resilient as Satan tries to get us to forget that we are righteous only through Jesus.

Pastor Paul LeBoutillier describes fighting spiritual battles this way:

> The enemy knows how to play mind games. And he will replay the little videotape in your head of all the creepy, crawly things you've ever done in your life. All the things you've ever said, all the things that disqualify you from God's love, and grace, and power. And they do disqualify you, apart from Jesus."[1]

Satan tries to convince us that our acceptance by God is dependent on us, on how good we are, on what we accomplish for Him; however, when we are wearing the breastplate of Christ's righteousness, we will recognize his lies.

Helmet of Salvation

No matter what comes against us, the helmet of God's armor reminds us of our salvation and that we belong to Christ. Remember that this is God's own armor. In Isaiah 59:17, we see that God "*put on righteousness as his breastplate, and the helmet of salvation on his head.*" This is not our armor we are putting on. This helmet is not ours. God has given it to us so that we can stand firm in this spiritual battle; in other

Scripture passages, Paul tells us to put on this armor. In Romans 13:12–14, he refers to it as the "*armor of light*" and commands us to "*clothe yourself with the Lord Jesus.*" We have taken off our old way of life and have put on Christ (Galatians 3:26–27). When we put on this armor, we also put on the mind of Christ (Philippians 2:5). Through the power of the Holy Spirit, we allow Him to live His life in and through us. When we put on His armor, we put on Christ.

Although I have the helmet of salvation available to me, I often choose to wear something else on my head. I put on a "helmet" that condemns me, filling my mind with words that denounce, blame, and even swear at me. These "helmets" immerse my thoughts with disapproval and criticism. When I do not put on God's helmet of salvation, my mind is clouded by guilt, shame, and fear, even the fear of losing my salvation. I must do what Jerry Bridges advised in *The Discipline of Grace*: "Preach the gospel to yourself every day."[2] I need the protection that the whole armor of God provides. The pieces of His armor are all "synonyms for the gospel. Translated literally from the Greek, they are: . . . the salvation . . . the justification . . . the truth . . . the gospel of peace . . . the faith . . . [and the] . . . word of God."[3] Without the "gospel armor,"[4] I am vulnerable. I need to be armed from the top of my head to the tips of my toes. I put on this armor when I preach the gospel message to myself: because God loves me so much, He sent His son Jesus to remove the separation between us caused by my sin. He took it with Him to the cross and forgave me of it all, offering me salvation and a new life, not because of what I do, but as a free gift. Now, there is no condemnation because as a new creation, I live through His power. Each day as we put on the helmet of salvation, we remind ourselves of this gospel because we are aware that we have an enemy who will attempt to penetrate our thoughts with lies and bombard us with uncertainty, doubt, and fear.

He will try to convince us to put on a different helmet. If we do, our Berry Bush will spread its branches, which will fill out with added berries, and soon our root lie will be so deep and hidden we won't even realize it's there.

Shoes of Peace

When I was a young girl, I really wanted a pair of popular tennis shoes called Zips. The commercials assured me that I would be able to run fast and have excellent traction. I remember the day my mom took me to the shoe store, and I found a pair in my size. They were just like I had dreamed of having. I snatched them off the shelf, and as my mom laced them up on my feet, I assured her that these shoes would make me super-fast. I took off running down the store aisle, shouting to my mom, "Look how fast I can run now!" Then I would abruptly stop, showing her the impressive traction that the shoes offered. Had this happened in today's world, I'm sure I would be a meme now, but these shoes made my little eight-year-old self believe that I genuinely did have a superpower.

When we put on God's shoes, we will have His superpower of peace. "*For shoes, put on the peace that comes from the Good News so that you will be fully prepared*" (Ephesians 6:15 NLT). The gospel of peace has us ready to handle whatever comes our way and to share the good news. We know we have laced up and tied our gospel of peace shoes securely when we patiently endure and support each other. Even when it is challenging in our community, we are committed to "*diligently keeping the unity of the Spirit with the peace that binds us*" (Ephesians 4:3 HCSB). These shoes of peace bring steadiness and sure-footedness that will enable us to stand firm, prepared, and in position for battle. We stand firm on the good news that we now have peace with God through the death and resurrection of Jesus. Because He loves us, He died in our place and conquered death. There is nothing that separates us from His love. He accepts us. He is trustworthy. He is in control of everything. He is our peace. It is His peace that gives us balance. When something unexpected hits us, our footing is secure. Wearing God's spiritual shoes brings peace. Our state of mind will not be clouded by fear or doubt. However, if in this spiritual battle we do not wear God's shoes, we will not be prepared to stand firm in the face of anxiety. When worry, fear, and disappointment approach, they will begin to overwhelm us. We will lose our footing and fall. That is when our berries will multiply. Lies about who God is will turn over in our head and persuade us not to trust Him. Our root lies will gain strength, grow deeper, corrode our self-talk, negate our testimony of God's peace, and impact our unity with other believers. These berries will keep us from standing firm together.

Listening for Truth

1. How would it change the way that you deal with difficult people if you remembered that this is a spiritual battle that we fight and that you are not struggling against flesh and blood? (Ephesians 6:12).
2. When have your thoughts persuaded you to loosen your armor and rely on your own righteousness?
3. Describe a helmet that you have chosen to wear instead of the helmet of salvation.
4. How will you preach the gospel to yourself every day?

Chapter 6

HOW TO STAND TOGETHER AGAINST SATAN

We often feel like we are all by ourselves. We feel our struggles are unique and more severe than the struggles of those around us. We think our situation is exclusive to us. We wage war in our minds. We know we have an enemy, but often feel like we must battle him alone. Last year, I taught high school American history at our homeschool co-op. In class, we learned about various wars with specific battles and important soldiers. One observation that we made is that none of these battles were fought with any one single soldier fighting by himself. All the battles involved an army, a team of soldiers working together. As followers of Christ, we are a part of a squad, platoon, company, battalion, brigade, division, corps . . . we are a member of the whole armed forces. This fact is important because as we consider wearing our spiritual armor and standing against the devil's schemes, we realize that we are a part of a team. We are not standing alone. However, that is how I feel. I view this armor as just for me, something I need to wear in my own battles that I face all by myself. I am wrong. This armor is not merely for me to fight all alone. This is a war that all of Christ's followers are a part of. All of us need to be wearing God's armor and standing together. We need our fellow warriors to stand beside us in this battle.

Picture the Roman shield; it was as large as a door. The warrior could completely hide behind it. It was most effective when the soldiers combined their shields and fought as a group. Standing shoulder to shoulder, the soldiers could interlock their shields and create an enclosure around themselves, called a *testudo*[1] ("tortoise") covering the top, sides, and front of their formation. Together, they became impenetrable. In the same way, as my community and I stand together and fight this spiritual battle, we will become impregnable. Together, I will not only benefit from my own shield but also from my fellow soldiers holding up their shields beside me.

Shield of Faith

We've been told we need to hold up our faith like a shield to protect us from the enemy's tactics, but what does that mean? How do we acquire faith, and where does it come from? The Bible explains to us that faith comes from God (Ephesians 2:8). Romans 10:17 describes how "*faith comes from hearing, that is, hearing the Good News about Christ*" (NLT). Faith comes from hearing, reading, and meditating on God's Word—from actively engaging our hearts and minds with Scripture. This is pivotal because it means faith does not originate within us. It is formed and strengthened by God's truth, not our own efforts. How freeing is that? It is not self-generated, as if I could will myself to be full of faith. I have often thought that if I just clenched my fists, closed my eyes, and believed really, really, hard, faith would come from within me. But the Bible explains the path. Faith is nurtured through my engagement with Him. Faith is an action, a choice. When doubt and fear approach us, we decide to pick up this shield and use our faith as a weapon. We choose to take up the shield of faith, holding up the things that we know to be true about God. Our lives will show that we believe in Him because we live like we believe in Him.

With the shield of faith, we have the power to "*extinguish all the flaming arrows of the evil one*" (Ephesians 6:16). The Roman soldier kept the leather covering his shield damp, prepared so that it would be ready to snuff out the firebombs sent from the enemy. In the same way, by taking up our shield of faith every day, we can "douse the doubt around us."[2] Our enemy tries to distract us by the flames. He wants us to become preoccupied, causing us to lose focus and become sidetracked. His doubt-filled darts are ablaze with the fire of insecurity, accusations, condemnations, and lies that produce in us anxiety, worry, and fear. The intent of these flaming arrows is to disable us from holding up faith. The Berry Bush grows bigger and stronger when we fail to hold up our faith. We will be too distracted to recognize the lies as we frantically deal with the flaming arrows catching us ablaze. As a result, growing underneath, hidden in the dark with our fears, is the lie that our opposer has been scheming to cultivate. He has gotten us to distrust God. That root lie about God's character will flourish and infect our thoughts, creating a barrier between us and God.

There is a barrier berry growing on my bush that keeps me from holding up the shield of faith. As I was writing this chapter, I realized this and consequently have been working to dig down to the root lie. The plump berry hangs off the branch, taunting me. It carries within it the thought that when there is something uncomfortable to talk about, I can't lead those conversations. I feel unequipped and all alone. Whether it is a challenging conversation with a coworker or family member, disunity at church, or any number of the cultural issues that are affecting us and our relationships, immediately, I hear in my head, "You can't do this. It's too hard. Just let it go." My stomach drops, and I break out in a sweat just thinking about it.

A recent experience highlighted this feeling even more for me. The other day, I realized that talking with my neighbors had become a berry on my bush. Can I be honest about something? Sometimes, my breathing becomes shallow, my chest tightens, and my heart pounds when there is a conversation about race relations. These discussions about race, culture, and heritage can feel especially weighty right now. It's impossible to ignore how much tension exists in the US, how quickly conversations can become emotionally charged, how easily misunderstandings can arise and deepen divides, and how much pain people carry connected to these topics.

I began to see how this tension affected me when I realized I had started avoiding my neighbors and feeling shame whenever I saw them. I want to be even more vulnerable here. It all started when their child came over to play. I asked her about her culture, but I mixed up her parents' nationalities. As a little girl, she didn't know how to answer my question and began to seem uncomfortable. I was embarrassed when I realized how my question might have made her feel, and my offense at confusing her family's heritage. I just let it drop and never said anything to her parents. As my husband and I were taking a walk the other night, we passed by their house, and I shared my berry with him. It was difficult to admit, as are all berries. I was surprised when he confessed that he too struggles with a similar berry. He discovered that it really ripens when he has challenging conversations, especially around culturally complex and weighty topics. For years, he avoided the awkward conversations. They made him uncomfortable because he felt like those types of delicate conversations fell outside his skill set. I realized then that the thoughts and feelings I was confronting were not mine alone. There is both spoken and unspoken pressure for our words to be perfectly formed, and in my conversation with this child, I stumbled on mine. Honestly, moments like that make it easy to freeze. I can feel the weight of it all before I even begin. I'm aware of how easily something could be misunderstood or taken in a way I never intended. That heaviness settles in, making the whole thing feel harder to navigate than it should, like trudging along a treacherous trail in the mountains, slipping and getting muddier with each soggy step.

As Paul and I talked, we asked each other why we are afraid of conversations that make us uncomfortable and began to unearth the root of our berries. We knew that deep down, we were believing a lie about God. Continuing to ask the question "Why?" got us to the place where we recognized the lie: God is not with us in these moments. This avoidance comes from a root lie that God is not trustworthy. He will not fulfill His promise never to leave or forsake us (Deuteronomy 31:6). Exposing that lie brings freedom. We realized that God's presence doesn't disappear when conversations get hard. Before He ascended to Heaven, Jesus reminded us, "*I am with you always*" (Matthew 28:20). And He explained that the Spirit of truth will be in us (John 14:16–17). We are never alone. He is with us and lives in us! There is no situation in which we should ever feel alone and afraid to talk about hard things. Because the Lord is with me and working inside me, I can enter into these difficult and uncomfortable conversations. They are too important to avoid. While some misunderstandings can still happen, I can be assured of God's presence with me. Now, when that berry shows up, and the poisonous thoughts invade my mind, I will recognize the root lie immediately. I will not fall for the lie but lean into the truth of Jesus's presence and trust His leading into the hard yet holy conversations.

I was sharing this thought with my friend Shannon, and she reminded me that "any hard conversation can be holy if we yield to the work and power of the Holy Spirit within us. And even if it still feels uncomfortable, it's okay." The woman at the well had a holy conversation with the Savior, but don't you think she felt uncomfortable when He brought up her five husbands (John 4:16–29)? Learning to be comfortable with being uncomfortable is the key to hard and holy conversations about race and culture. Willingly embracing growth opportunities rather than avoiding them begins in my mind. When I choose to set my thoughts firmly on the truth of who God is, I will hold up the shield of faith.

All About Unity

Because the battle takes place within my mind, I think that I don't need anyone else alongside me to fight. The powers of darkness want to convince me that not only am I stuck in a hopeless situation, but that I am all alone. Satan brings anxiety and tells me to isolate myself. My thoughts tell me, "I don't want to burden anyone with my problems." I ask myself, "What would others say if they knew I was struggling with this?" But I am wrong. My loneliness only makes my situation worse because I was not meant to try to cope with life's problems all by myself. I need others, and they need me. We need each other. We are called to live in unity despite any social, ethnic, or cultural barriers. As we consider Paul's metaphor of God's armor, we need to remember that he included the armor teaching in his letter to the church in Ephesus. The focus of Ephesians is all about unity. Christ has reconciled us to Himself and to each other. Now, through Jesus, we form one body. However, the spiritual powers of darkness do not want us to be one body. They are drawn up in battle array against the Church, with one goal: to corrode our unity. The Church is in a fight against evil rulers and authorities of this unseen world. In his book *How to Heal Our Racial Divide*, Derwin Gray points to an aspect of this hostility:

We are all born into conflict that we did not create. These disputes existed long before we arrived on planet earth, but we still have to live with their aftermath. . . . Our world is a battle zone that reeks of generational institutional discrimination and personal contempt.[3]

We are living in this combat area where the spiritual powers of evil are fighting to keep us divided. One of their most successful and detestable divisive schemes is discrimination. Showing prejudice and partiality is common in the church, but it should not be so. *"My dear brothers and sisters, how can you claim to have faith in our glorious Lord Jesus Christ if you favor some people over others?"* (James 2:1 NLT) James gives the example of showing favoritism to a wealthy person over a poor person. Galatians teaches us that the prejudicial distinctions that we make between race, gender, and social status have been obliterated. Christ has broken down the wall of hostility between people and has brought us together. Because we are followers of Jesus, oneness should be our goal. We should be contributing to bringing about reconciliation and unity. As followers of Jesus, how beautiful it is to read in 2 Corinthians 5:18–20 that we have the ministry of reconciliation. "*He gave us this wonderful message of reconciliation. So we are Christ's ambassadors*" (verse 20 NLT).

Together, we work to spread the good news that, through Christ, we can be restored to a right relationship with God and with each other. We must live this out. The Church is designed to be made up of every race, tribe, nation, and language (Revelation 7:9); yet we section ourselves off into divisions based on where we feel most comfortable. This calling doesn't remove the tension, but it does give us every reason to lean in. We have allowed racial and cultural differences to fracture the unity of the Body of Christ. I need to ask myself, am I guilty of participating in this division? Am I allowing berries to grow on my bush that are keeping me from the kind of unity Christ prayed that I would be a part of? We are fighting a spiritual war, and our enemy is unseen. We should not allow anything to separate us; we should stand together. Just as Jesus prayed to the Father for us: "*Protect them by the power of your name so that they will be united, just as we are*" (John 17:11 NLT).

Last night, our church celebrated Good Friday with a walk-through experience featuring interactive prayer stations. As I walked through the steps of Jesus to the Cross, I began to think about how Satan chose to attack Him. It wasn't just one person screaming, "Crucify him," it wasn't a lone assassin that Satan used to murder Jesus while He was in the garden praying. No, the devil used the corrupt religious and political system. Today, the powers of darkness continue to operate this way, and often, we blame other humans; we do not recognize the unseen powers at work. We point fingers at each other.

I loved teaching that American History class and still reflect on many of our classroom discussions today. Occasionally, I would ask them, "Which ideas from our nation's history can you still see influencing life in the United States today?" Looking back is important so that we can parse through our story, our systems, and the events of our nation's history. Doing so invites an honest reflection on how those patterns from the past still shape our world today. The Declaration of Independence declared that all men are created equal, yet from that very moment, our society excluded half the men and every woman, forgetting that all people bear the image of God. That error eventually led to the Civil War, and its repercussions continue to this day. The corrupt political system oppressed and divided. Racism was normalized. As recent as sixty years ago, segregation was still a legal practice. All of society was tainted by it, and even the church became defined by the race of its members. The effect of that can still be seen today. Sadly, when I was growing up in Texas, there were basically three churches: a White church, a Black church, and a Hispanic church. Although we all worshipped the same Lord and Savior, we did not choose to worship together. Today, it is different; in many churches, we are striving to become one in our diversity, but we have a long way to go to truly be the expression of the body of Christ. Because we live in a society whose past and present still bear the marks of racism, berries have developed on our bushes that have created division where Christ intends oneness. These berries have corrupted our thoughts and have kept us from honoring our brothers and sisters in Christ's love. Our unification is necessary to fight this battle. We must stand hand in hand against the spiritual powers of evil. We need to get rid of these berries, remove the root, and stand together.

Not that long ago, I took a Bible class. For the final project, the instructor assigned a meditative artistic piece that communicated how a passage in Ephesians had challenged my community and me to respond. I wrote a song and chose Ephesians chapter 4: "*There is one body, one Spirit—just as you were called to the one hope that belongs to your call—one Lord, one faith, one baptism, one God and Father over all*" (Ephesians 4:4–6 ESV). Here is my song:

Verse 1
Once we were so far away from Him,
Then out of two, He created one new man.
Being built together has always been His plan
Into a holy temple, through His Spirit, as only He can.

Chorus
One Body,
One Spirit,
One hope that we are called to,
One God and Father over all.

Verse 2
Oneness, but we're so different, how can it be?
His sacrifice to bring us unity
All the while we're livin' separately
Deceiving ourselves that we're living for Christ only.

Bridge
But we're not living a life
Worthy of the calling.
How can we be still so divided
With our hearts this blinded?
'Cause that wall of hostility
Jesus broke it down.
He's our peace, and He prays for our unity.

Verse 3
One body. Look around you, what do you see?
We're the church, members of one family.

Then why is it one sits in comfort while the other hurts?
When Christ's death has reconciled all the earth.
When Christ's death has reconciled all the earth!

Jesus prayed for our oneness. He prayed in John 17 that we would be brought to complete unity, made perfectly one, so that the world would know of His love for us. When we decide to follow Christ, we become part of His body, the Church, which consists of everyone, all over the world, every person who loves and follows Jesus. As His body, the Church relies on all its individual members, each with their different gifts and roles. Everyone is essential and valuable (1 Corinthians 12:12). We are all one in God's eyes. As a body, if one part suffers, the whole body suffers. By ourselves, we are like that example of a lone piece of coal that, when near all the other pieces of coal, is part of the fire, but by itself, the red-hot ember grows dull and gray. Eventually, it becomes cold until it is put back into the blaze with the other embers.

When we are living alongside other Christians, our faith will be strengthened. Together, leaning into the power of Christ, we will meet our fears head-on. Excavating the root lies of your Berry Bush is best done through community. We need to help each other ask the necessary questions that will lead us back to our root lie. It is very difficult to get to our lie beneath the lies alone. We prefer to figure things out on our own because it is hard to be vulnerable with each other. We don't want to expose our inner thoughts and sins to our brothers and sisters in Christ; however, we will miss all that God has for us if we fail to benefit from the process of learning in community. Exploring together offers us significant advantages: all kinds of giftings, abilities, knowledge, and cultural experiences together under the lordship of Christ. We are empowered as we learn from and understand each other through the lens of the gospel.[4] When we come together to help one another find out what lies beneath the lies we are believing, new questions will emerge, ones that we haven't thought of on our own. When we live out James 5:16, "*Confess your sins to each other and pray for each other,*" mutual transparency and accountability will be normalized, and that will foster unity. Because we may have a blind spot that keeps us from the kind of unity with Christ we long for, going through the Berry Bush together with other trusted Christ followers will be an integral part of finding freedom. Recently, I went through the Berry Bush exercise with some coworkers, and afterward, as we talked it over, one comment that resonated with everyone was how helpful it was to share our root lies with one another. By mutual confession, we showed each other how we all struggle with lies about who God is. We need each other to dig down deep to find our lie underneath and encourage one another to live in the truth.

Sword of the Spirit

As we stand together in community, we utilize the weapon that Paul calls the "sword of the Spirit." This blade will have the devil on the defensive. The Holy Spirit teaches us how to wield God's Word so that we can push back evil forces, fortify our hearts, and bring freedom. The sword depicted here is like a dagger, used for close hand-to-hand combat. We use God's Word to fight off Satan's schemes, just like Jesus did in the desert. Because the Holy Spirit lives inside those who follow Christ, He will help us when our adversary sends thoughts into our minds designed to lead us away from Christ. It is essential to have Scripture hidden in your heart for those moments. When you began to follow Jesus, He gave you the Holy Spirit as a helper who "*will teach you all things and will remind you of everything*" in His Word (John 14:26). You have the Holy Spirit, who will help you recall specific Scripture to combat Satan's lies.

However, if you have never read or memorized His Word, how will you recall it? To fight off the spiritual forces of evil, you must fill your mind with the Word of God. Part of the process after you have finished the Berry Bush exercise is to create a Truth Tree. This is where you will find those parts of God's Word that will combat your root lie about God. These verses will remind you how much God loves you, cherishes you, and cares for you. You will use Scripture to meditate on God's goodness, faithfulness, and sovereignty. It is His character that has been under attack. For that reason, the verses we will choose for our Truth Trees will reflect His character.

I have tried memorizing Scripture on my own and have had some success, but the times I have done it in community have benefited me the most. Together, we help each other to remember and hold each other accountable. I can still hear the Texas twang of a college buddy as we worked together to memorize Ephesians 3:14. His drawl could really draw out the phrase "Put on Looooove." The verses we've memorized as a family have really stuck; maybe it is because of the kids' fun hand motions or the music. I love to sing them. Most likely, they are easier to remember because sharing in learning together created a deeper emotional experience that strengthened the neural connections and thus made the verses stick. Because we believe that God's Word is the most effective weapon against our anxiety, fears, and worries, as a church body, we need to make memorizing Scripture a priority. We know that this weapon is powerful. It will transform us! Hebrews 4:12 describes Scripture as "*alive and active. Sharper than any double-edged sword, it penetrates even to dividing soul and spirit, joints and marrow; it judges the thoughts and attitudes of the heart.*" When you saturate your mind with God's truth, you will see from His perspective. Once you shift your focus from self, you will experience His hope, joy, and peace as you stand together in unity, stand ready with the Word of God, and stand in prayer.

Listening for Truth

1. Those flaming arrows the devil shoots at us become our berries. Name one flaming arrow you're constantly having to extinguish. What are you doing to "douse the doubt?" How is it working?
2. What berry might be growing on your bush that is keeping you from living out the kind of oneness that Jesus prayed for us?
3. Digging up root lies is best done with others. What does your community look like right now? If you want to grow in this area, what steps could you take to develop deeper community?
4. List three things that you can do to **stand together** against Satan.

Chapter 7

STAND IN PRAYER AND BE FLABBERGASTED

Sometimes, when we pray, we are absolutely flabbergasted by the way the Lord answers. One morning as my family sat around the breakfast table, I picked up a devotional book by Patricia St. John.[1] In it, she shares the story of two sisters, Fatima and Mary, who ministered in India, providing medicine and sharing stories of Jesus. After spending a late night proclaiming the gospel in a remote village, they set out early the next morning on a market bus for part of the long journey home. When they reached the place where they hoped to get off, the driver refused to stop, insisting on continuing to the next bridge. Frustrated by the miles this would add to their journey home, Mary prayed for the bus to stop, but it did not.

When the bus finally did stop, they were still many miles from home. Discouraged, they wondered what to do next. As they debated, a woman approached carrying a sick baby. Much to their surprise, the woman said she had dreamed of a man dressed in white who told her to bring her sick child to a nurse at the road by the bridge.

Realizing God's purpose, the sisters walked to their home with the mother, treated the baby, and she recovered fully. Later, they visited the mother and baby and shared the gospel. They all thanked God for answering no to Mary's prayer and accomplishing something far greater than they had ever imagined.

When we order our lives around God's desires, the way we live our lives will become like a prayer. When we pray, "Your will be done," we should anticipate that we will be flabbergasted by the way He answers.

Stand in Prayer

We are called to stand in prayer. Paul concludes his description of spiritual armor by emphasizing the crucial role of prayer in this spiritual battle. He is adamant about praying. Five times he emphasizes prayer in Ephesians 6:18–20 (emphasis mine):

> *And* ***pray*** *in the Spirit on all occasions with all kinds of* ***prayers*** *and requests. With this in mind, be alert and always keep on* ***praying*** *for all the Lord's people.* ***Pray*** *also for me, that whenever I speak, words may be given me so that I will fearlessly make known the mystery of the gospel, for which I am an ambassador in chains.* ***Pray*** *that I may declare it fearlessly, as I should.*

Prayer is a vital part of this spiritual war. We are instructed as believers to be alert, but being watchful is a struggle because the devil is doing everything he can to distract, tempt, and bring doubt to stop us from praying. Notice how Paul stresses "*all occasions*" and "*all kinds of prayers.*" Praying is a way of life. When we live constantly in the awareness of God's presence, we will be compelled to talk with

Him throughout the day, on every occasion, as the Spirit leads with all kinds of prayers and requests.

My pastor preached a sermon on this passage recently and emphasized being consistent and persistent in prayer so that we have the endurance necessary for the fight. He gave the analogy that prayer is to the Christian what water is to the boxer. During a match, the boxer returns to their corner every three minutes and stays there for sixty seconds. They take that break to breathe, get healed, get hyped, and, most importantly, rehydrate. The water in their corner is essential to their success in the fight. During a typical three-minute match, a boxer can lose one to two percent of their body mass in water. If they fight with a three- to five-percent loss, they will enter the phase of dehydration. The lack of water can cause them to lose the fight, as dehydration slows their ability to think and act. As their bodies lose endurance, they drop their guard and are unprepared for the knockout punch. Prayer is our "spiritual hydration"[2] in the middle of this battle. Just like the boxer's sixty-second break, it doesn't take long for us to go to the corner to breathe, get healed, get hyped, and rehydrate through prayer.

We are told to "*pray in the Spirit*" (Ephesians 6:18). Jesus told His disciples He was leaving but promised the gift of the Holy Spirit. This promise signifies God's presence and power within us. The gift of His Spirit empowers us to participate in this war. Philip Yancey explains, "He went away for our sakes, as a form of power sharing, to invite us into direct communion with God and to give us a crucial role in the struggle against the forces of evil."[3] We play an essential part in this battle because, as we pray, the Holy Spirit will guide our prayers. We ask the Spirit to enable us to pray about what is really going on. The Spirit will prompt us and help us to pray with boldness according to God's will. We pray in submission to God, not simply sharing our thoughts and our desires, but coming from a place of complete dependence. There have been times when I know I should pray, but I don't have words. I don't know what to say, and I feel like I can't even gather my thoughts to form a cohesive thought to pray. In those moments when we are so beaten down and discouraged from the battle, we should recall Paul's words:

> *The Spirit helps us in our weakness. We do not know what we ought to pray for, but the Spirit himself intercedes for us with groans that words cannot express. And he who searches our hearts knows the mind of the Spirit, because the Spirit intercedes for the saints in accordance with God's will.*
>
> —Romans 8:26–27

Are You Allergic to Helplessness?

As I was in the middle of writing this chapter, I was hit from out of the blue with a virus that knocked me off my feet. I had a case of vertigo so crippling that I could not get out of bed. I could not do anything for myself. No matter how much I willed my body to get over it, I was stuck there. I was out of town on a trip and all alone. I needed help! Thankfully, the Lord had seen to it that a friend's trip was delayed, so she was unable to travel and could be there to care for me. She had to bring me food, water, medicine, and attend to me. I was totally dependent. I was helpless. I didn't like it, but it did get me thinking about the connection between helplessness and prayer. Those times when I have felt the least in control and most afraid are the times that my cries to God have been like a child's. In his book *The Praying Life,* Paul Miller explains that we all need to acknowledge our helplessness. He shares:

> Little children are good at helplessness. It's what they do best. But as adults, we soon forget how important helplessness is. I for one, am allergic to helplessness. I don't like it. I want a plan, an idea, or maybe a friend to listen to my problem. This is how I instinctively approach everything because I am confident in my own abilities. . . . God wants us to come to him empty-handed, weary, and heavy-laden. Instinctively, we want to get rid of our helplessness before we come to God.[4]

Sometimes, when it comes to how we pray, we think we know what to pray. We know what God needs to fix and how He should fix it. We want to handle life ourselves, and often we come to God trying to help Him figure out the answer. However, Paul Miller offers this perspective:

> The gospel, God's free gift of grace in Jesus, only works when we realize we don't have it all together. The same is true for prayer. The very thing we are allergic to—our helplessness—is what makes prayer work. It works because we are helpless. We can't do life on our own.[5]

God wants us to bring all of ourselves to Him, our helplessness and weaknesses. He doesn't want us to try to hide any part of ourselves from Him. He already knows every mistake and disappointment, and still He longs for us to share our lives with Him. He wants to give us His power and strength. He does that through prayer.

Paul asks the Ephesians to pray for him. He could have asked them to pray that he would be freed from prison and all charges dropped, but he didn't. Instead, he asked that words would be given to him and that he would have the courage to continue to speak boldly for Christ. He knew God was in control and trusted in God's goodness, whether he was in jail or not. His prayer request was that he would fearlessly declare the gospel. I wonder what my prayer request would be in that situation. This is a lesson for me as I consider my Berry Bush. Many of my berries have to do with being afraid of going through difficult circumstances. Paul certainly had his share of difficulties and had already dealt with his berries. He tells us that he asked God three times to remove a thorn in his flesh. He called it a "*messenger of Satan*," but God replied, "*My grace is all you need. My power works best in weakness*" (2 Corinthians 12:9a NLT). Through all the hardships he experienced, Paul learned not to listen to the lies. He had roots that fed him truths such as: God loves me, God is trustworthy, God is in control. Because he chose to listen to the truth about who God is, Paul could confidently say, "*I am glad to boast about my weaknesses, so that the power of Christ can work through me*" (2 Corinthians 12:9b NLT).

As we take up our spiritual armor, we pray. We acknowledge that every battle we face is actually God's battle, not ours. Only through His strength and His mighty power can we come against the devil's schemes. We pray because God is offering us the opportunity to join Him in what He is doing. We pray so that we can take off our old self and clothe ourselves with Christ. Paul tells us to be strong in God's strength, not our own. We pray to have His strength so that we will be able to stay alert and stand firm. The way to be strong in the Lord is to put on His armor, and the only way to do that is through prayer. All over the Bible, we see people calling on the name of the Lord. Throughout Scripture, we are given instructions to pray. Jesus even taught us how to pray. We will cover that prayer in a few chapters, but for now, let's consider these questions: What would happen if we devoted ourselves to a persistent and consistent prayer life? What would our Berry Bush look like? How big would our berries be? Would we have as many berries as we do now? Would anxiety consume us as it does now, or would we resist Satan by refusing to open the door and put a welcome mat out for him?

Listening for Truth

1. What would praying as a way of life look like for you?
2. Think about a time that you were flabbergasted by the way God answered your prayers.
3. As you consider your berries growing on your Berry Bush, do you have any berries that are growing because of a fear of going through difficult circumstances? If so, why do you think they are growing?
4. Think about the phrase, "Every battle we face is actually God's battle, not ours." Do you agree? Why or why not? How does this impact your prayer life?

Chapter 8

HOW YOU PUT OUT THE WELCOME MAT FOR SATAN

When she was a baby, our daughter had lots of health problems. We had several different therapists come into our home to help us care for her. Her occupational therapist and I became friends, and on a particularly heavy emotional day, I told her that although at that moment everything seemed overwhelming, I was trying to trust God through it. She got in my face and admonished me with her finger wagging, "Don't try to give me that 'God won't give you more than you can bear' crap!" I promised her that I wasn't, because obviously I already had more than I could handle. I needed Jesus to help me. She wasn't a follower of Jesus and couldn't really understand my reasoning, but she was aware of the verse that many of her patients' parents had quoted to her: "*No temptation has overtaken you except what is common to mankind. And God is faithful; he will not let you be tempted beyond what you can bear*" (1 Corinthians 10:13). This verse talks about temptation and God giving us a way out of it. It does not mean that God will not allow us to suffer more than we think we can bear. It is quite likely that we will suffer more than we think we can bear. We wouldn't be able to measure how much we think we can handle, anyway, or have the audacity to advise God, "Oh no! This pain is too much. I am at capacity for what I can bear. No more!" Instead, we recognize that relying on His strength is the only way to get us through it. God will allow hardships and trials beyond your ability to manage on your own; however, these trials are not beyond His ability. In every moment, He promises to give you His strength so that you can endure. He may give you more than you can handle, but not more than He can. The Apostle Paul testified to the Corinthian church the truth of how suffering can be beyond our power and ability to bear:

> *We think you ought to know, dear brothers and sisters, about the trouble we went through in the province of Asia. We were crushed and overwhelmed beyond our ability to endure, and we thought we would never live through it. In fact, we expected to die. But as a result, we stopped relying on ourselves and learned to rely only on God, who raises the dead.*
>
> —2 Corinthians 1:8–9 NLT

God does allow affliction that is more than we can endure because He doesn't want us to rely on ourselves, but on Him. That overwhelming feeling is what drives us to seek God. Now that you see where these poisonous berries come from, instead of continuing in the destructive thought cycle, you can take that anxious thought and allow it to steer you toward the truth about

God. Consider how 1 Corinthians 10:3 reads in the New Living Translation:

> *The temptations in your life are no different from what others experience. And God is faithful. He will not allow the temptation to be more than you can stand. When you are tempted, he will show you a way out so that you can endure.*

From this translation, we see that the allure of sin is common. All of humanity confronts it. Others have been tempted just like you have, and by God's grace, overcame it. You can too. You might feel like you are the only one who faces a particular temptation and that you cannot get a hold of it or get it under control. You want victory, but feel defeated, ready to throw in the towel and just live with it, excusing yourself from continuing in the fight and resigned to the fact that you fought but couldn't win. Look again at this verse and remind yourself of the truth: God is faithful! He is promising you a way out of temptation. "There will never be a sin that is inevitable. The temptation is inevitable, but the sin is not."[1] God promises to strengthen you when temptation comes and to provide a way out so you can endure. This is not in your own strength. It doesn't come from within yourself. It comes only from Christ. He will make a way, but you have to choose to take it. When you refuse His way of escape, you leave yourself vulnerable to the enemy.

Satan Wants Our Minds

Throughout Scripture, we hear the warning that the devil is scheming and, through his conniving ways, is plotting to deceive us and lead us astray. He is aiming to undermine our relationship with God. His goal is to lead us away from God, persuading us through our own thoughts. He wants our minds. John Mark Comer, in his book *Live No Lies*, shares the story of a fourth-century AD intellectual named Evagrius Ponticus, who wrote about his strategy for overcoming the devil. Comer points out:

> The most surprising feature of Evagrius's paradigm is his claim that the fight against demonic temptation is a fight against what he called *logismoi*—a Greek word that can be translated as "thoughts," "thought patterns," your "internal narratives," or "internal belief structures." They are the content of our thought lives and the mental markers by which we navigate life. For Evagrius, these logismoi weren't *just* thoughts; they were thoughts with a malignant will behind them, a dark animating force of evil.[2]

Believers beware! The devil is after our thoughts, and we give him so many opportunities without even realizing what we are doing.

Pay Attention!

When I was a little girl, I was often immersed in my own imaginary world, not aware of what was going on around me. My father would call out, "Pay attention!" to remind me to be aware of my surroundings, stay in tune and present, and watch for steps, obstacles, and other people. There were also times when he advised me to pay attention to myself so that I would realize how my words, tone, and attitude were affecting others. I was your typical baby of the family with a precocious attitude who was self-assertive and overconfident. I thought I knew everything and often spoke my mind without considering my words or their impact. My father had to remind me so often that as I grew older, the words "Pay attention" became a bit of a joke between us. The other day, I was reading in Luke and found Jesus telling the disciples the same thing:

> *Temptations to sin are sure to come, but woe to the one through whom they come! It would be better for him if a millstone were hung around his neck and he were cast into the sea than that he should cause one of these little ones to sin.* ***Pay attention to yourselves!*** *If your brother sins, rebuke him, and if he repents, forgive him, and if he sins against you seven times in the day, and turns to you seven times, saying, 'I repent,' you must forgive him." The apostles said to the Lord, "Increase our faith!" And the Lord said, "If you had faith like a grain of mustard seed, you could say to this mulberry tree, 'Be uprooted and planted in the sea,' and it would obey you.*
>
> —Luke 17:1–6 ESV (emphasis mine)

"*Pay attention to yourselves!*" Jesus wants us to be prepared and warns us to expect temptations. He tells us there is a 100 percent chance that snares and traps are coming, so He expects us to be vigilant in our personal walk. He also warns us not to be the cause of temptation, but to be careful about how we live our lives and how we influence the people around us. We need to be mindful of how our choices and reactions impact those who are vulnerable. Our calling is to support and build each other up, not cause others to fall in their faith.

The strong imagery Jesus uses with the millstone conveys a serious warning. "*Pay attention to yourself!*" He is calling us to be self-aware and alert, on guard against temptation. He directs us to protect others by putting them first so that we do not cause them to sin by our unwillingness to forgive. Forgiveness is an expression of God's character. When we forgive others, we are relying on God's power. Will we show love in return when we are offended? Even though we have been hurt and insulted, He does not give us a pass on forgiveness. "*Anyone who loves a fellow believer is living in the light and does not cause others to stumble*" (1 John 2:10 NLT). When we love, we live in a way that reveals the light of Christ, and we will not cause others to sin. Romans 14:13 tells us to "*stop passing judgment on one another. Instead, make up your mind not to put any stumbling block or obstacle in your brother's way.*" We need to check our actions and attitudes, prioritizing others' spiritual health by loving them like Christ loves us. How can we accept His forgiveness but not extend forgiveness to others? Because He has forgiven us, Jesus is calling us to always offer forgiveness.

Forgiveness to the Extreme

Jesus takes forgiveness to the extreme by declaring that even if someone sins against you seven times a day, you must forgive them. This is the kind of forgiveness that you must keep giving over and over again. The disciples responded to this challenge with, "*Increase our faith!*" Forgiving that much seems impossible because bitterness and unforgiveness can have such deep pieces of our hearts. With this example, Jesus made it crystal clear that forgiveness is ultimately between God and me. Remember, after He taught the disciples the model prayer, He stated matter-of-factly, "*If you forgive men when they sin against you, your heavenly Father will also forgive you. But if you do not forgive men their sins, your Father will not forgive your sins*" (Matthew 6:14–15). Unforgiveness in my heart is denying that I am a sinner. When you offend me, you are a sinner committing a sin against me, another sinner. But when I sin against God, I am a sinner committing a sin against the righteous, pure, and holy God. Jesus is explaining that our forgiveness is connected to God. No matter what offense has been done to me, it doesn't compare at all to what I have done to God. Notice how each time God urges us to forgive others, He points us back to His own generous forgiveness toward us.

"Give us more faith!" the disciples pleaded with Jesus. Looking around, Jesus points to a tree and says, "*If you have faith as small as a mustard seed, you can say to this mulberry tree, 'Be uprooted and planted in the sea,' and it will obey you*" (Luke 17:6). Jesus directs their attention to a type of tree that has an extensive root system with one of the deepest root structures. Because of these deep roots, it would be a humongous task to try to remove the tree. To top it off, He says to plant it in the sea of all places! He informs them that all this requires only a little bit of faith, so small that He compares it to the tiniest of all seeds. It is as if He is saying, "You simply need to have faith to forgive, just some faith to forgive. You don't need more faith." It is not the amount of faith but the object of our faith that matters. If God is the object of our faith, then He will move the tree. When we think about freeing ourselves from deeply rooted bitterness and resentment, it seems unimaginable. Our anger and hostility continue to feed our unforgiveness. We get stuck in unforgiveness, and it is the worst kind of slavery because it is a self-created prison.[3] When someone hurts me, I blame them for my bitterness. I feel like I am punishing them by holding onto resentment, but in reality, I am punishing myself. It is my response that has kept me imprisoned. I have not made the connection between my forgiveness and God's forgiveness. I have not considered how much He is forgiving me every single day. He forgives. He is a "forgiver." If we follow Him, we will be "forgivers" too.[4]

By choosing to forgive, we are not minimizing what we have suffered or dismissing our pain. We are inviting the Lord into our pain. Repressing our feelings is not the answer; we need to express our hurt to the One who loves us most. "We invite God's closeness."[5] We surrender our suffering to Him. As we hand over our unforgiveness to the Lord, we also relinquish our right to judge the person who hurt us. We acknowledge that our unforgiveness is judgment and that we are not the final judge. Therefore, we lay all the offense at God's feet because He is the ultimate judge. When we choose to forgive and leave the judging to God, we release our entitlement to be angry and relinquish the right to justify our bitterness. He is the one who can uproot the unforgiveness in our hearts. As I begin to consider the berries of unforgiveness on my Berry Bush, it is apparent that I have believed a lie about Him. Still, Jesus tells me that it only takes a tiny bit of faith to forgive, to get way down deep, uproot the ugliness of that lie, and eradicate that barrier between Him and me.

"*Pay attention to yourselves!*" Jesus tells us too. This Berry Bush tool will help you do that. When you recognize a poisonous berry thought, you can quickly trace it down to its ugly root and stop yourself from continuing that thought pattern. For example, when I realized I was growing a berry of unforgiveness, I began to ask myself, "Why?" I worked bit by bit, dealing with pride and self-righteousness, to get down to my root lie about God's character and figured out that I was believing that God was not in control; therefore, I wanted to be in control. I wanted to be the judge. Realizing that the ugly lie was affecting me and becoming a barrier between God and me, I told myself the truth about forgiveness, the truth about the omnipotence of God.

Don't Give the Devil a Foothold

Jesus is serious about unforgiveness. When we experience personal conflict and do not resolve our differences, nurturing our anger and resentment, allowing it to fester, we put out a giant welcome mat inviting Satan into our minds. Let's heed the warning, "*don't sin by letting anger control you. Don't let the sun go down while you are still angry, for anger gives a foothold to the devil*" (Ephesians 4:26–27). When we harbor anger, we open ourselves up to bitterness. Because of the unresolved anger, shame will come, and so will our enemy. Continuing in our anger gives the devil a *foothold*, an opportunity to trick us with more lies. Louie Giglio wrote a book called, *Don't Give the Devil a Seat at Your Table.* In it, he talks about how he allowed the enemy access to his thoughts, attitudes, emotions, and perspective. He was having a conversation with a killer. He realized that, instead of joining God at the table He had prepared for them, Louie was inviting his adversary to sit down at it.[6] We are told to "*Resist the devil, and he will flee from you*" (James 4:7). Second Corinthians 2:11 teaches us to forgive and show love, "*so that Satan will not outsmart us for we are familiar with his evil schemes*" (NLT).

His schemes involve our thoughts, which we know lead to our feelings, behaviors, and eventually what we believe. Paul told the church in 2 Corinthians 11:3, "*But I am afraid that as the serpent deceived Eve by his cunning, your thoughts will be led astray from a sincere and pure devotion to Christ*" (ESV). He was concerned that their thoughts would be lured away, seduced by Satan to stop believing the truth about Christ. Look at the example of Ananias in Acts 5:3. Peter asked, "*Ananias, why did you let Satan fill you with the idea that you could deceive the Holy Spirit? You've held back some of the money you received for the land*" (GWT). Ananias, as he considered his circumstances and feelings, must have thought about it and rationalized why he needed to keep that extra money. He listened to Satan and fell prey. Stay alert and watch out! Satan's game plan is to manipulate our thoughts and drop seeds of doubt about God's character. Have you ever been tempted to doubt God's character based on what you were feeling in the moment, and the circumstances you were facing?

As we begin to doubt the character of God, we fall prey to another scheme that the devil especially loves to use: our pride. The Apostle Paul, in 1 Timothy 3:6–7, describes the kind of leaders God wants and intentionally points out how the devil seeks to trap us with conceit. All of us can act like the ass in that old Aesop fable,[7] who during a religious procession through town carried a sacred image on his back. As he made his way closer to the temple, he noticed people bowing their heads in reverence or falling to their knees as he passed by. Believing that the honor was being paid to him, the ass bristled with pride and began to bray loudly. With his head full of himself, he became so puffed up with conceit that he presumed he could do as he wished, so he stopped and declined to continue any farther, braying even louder. In the middle of his song, the driver began to beat him with a stick. "Get along, you stupid ass," he called out. "The honor is not meant for you, but for the image you are carrying." Let us not be like the ass, believing the lie of conceit, and allowing it to lead us down a path of arrogance that the devil will use, and we will regret. After all, "*God opposes the proud*" (James 4:6).

Our adversary wants to attack our minds and will capitalize on the normal, natural sexual desires that God has given us. Pornography is an example. According to Covenant Eyes, 64 percent of Christian men and 15 percent of Christian women say they watch porn at least once a month.[8] Satan is using these images to destroy our intimacy with God and each other. He lures us into seeking our own pleasure while objectifying precious people who are made in the image of God.

Our enemy's goal is to deceive us into thinking that our possessions and pursuits of this world will fulfill us. He uses our comfort to entice us. His scheming contorts and twists our understanding of true happiness. John Mark Comer shared this quote by Saint Ignatius of Loyola: "Sin is the unwillingness to trust that what God wants for me is only my deepest happiness."[9] Our enemy has convinced us that we cannot trust God because He does not care if we are happy. The devil has persuaded us to believe that sin is the solution to our unhappiness, making us blind to the truth that genuine happiness is only found in a relationship with Christ. We are living by the narratives of the world, and the Father of Lies seizes every opportunity to entangle our thoughts.

Prepare Your Minds for Battle

Our thoughts are where active fighting occurs. Knowing that these are the types of tricks Satan uses to go after our minds, we must be vigilant against giving the devil any opportunity to get the better of us. Do not listen to his lies but recognize them for what they are—the opposite of who God is. This is his oldest trick, and we are still falling for it. Do not be unaware of your thoughts. Prepare your mind for action and "*Gird up the loins of your mind*" (1 Peter 1:13 NKJV). What a mental image! Here, Peter uses a metaphor to exhort us to prepare our minds for action, stay alert, and be ready for anything. This gives us a visual of a Roman soldier tucking the loose ends of his tunic into his belt to free up his legs for easier movement in combat. God told the Israelites to do this exact thing the night before their escape from Egypt. They were to have their belts fastened while they ate the Passover meal (Exodus 12:11). This way, their legs would be unencumbered and ready to run. Loose thoughts are like that loose garment that could trip us up. We need God's belt of truth wrapped around us, holding us together and securing the loose thoughts that threaten to trip us up. Without His truth, reining in our wandering thoughts is impossible.

Truth needs to be the core of everything we think, do, and believe. As we gird up the loins of our mind, we prepare our minds for battle using the truth about God. As Jennie Allen reminds us in her book *Get Out of Your Head*, "The greatest spiritual battle of our generation is being fought between our ears."[10] Because the war is all about what we ponder, contemplate, and reason, this idea of taking every thought captive "isn't merely a helpful process to adopt. Don't forget. . . . this is an all-out war."[11] The battleground is our mind:

> *For though we live in the world, we do not wage war as the world does. The weapons we fight with are not the weapons of the world. On the contrary, they have divine power to demolish strongholds. We demolish arguments and every pretension that sets itself up against the knowledge of God, and we take captive every thought to make it obedient to Christ.*
>
> —2 Corinthians 10:3–5

We wage a different kind of war, a war for our minds. This fight will determine what we think about God. Doubts about who God is begin to rise in our minds. Negative thoughts about God's character start to form in us. Reasonings that contradict what we know about God begin to show up in our minds, and we begin entertaining ideas that challenge His character. That is why it is so important to uncover our root lies. Because if these arguments about God's character are reinforced in our actions, they will become a part of our belief system and strongholds in our lives. This is why we must take every thought captive, so that these ideas do not develop into sinful strongholds that create a rut in our hearts. That rut leads us around and around, far from the truth, and that is just what Satan wants.

Our adversary is after our minds. He attempts to influence and distract us from the truth about God, from the reality that Christ, through his death and resurrection, has paid the penalty for our sins, and we are now completely accepted, forgiven, and dearly loved. Tim Keller shared in a sermon how knowing and living out the gospel defeats Satan's strategies. He observed that the devil has "two basic strategies: temptation and accusation, but the Gospel message is the armor."[12] The accuser comes to us and seizes the opportunity to tempt us to look at ourselves instead of our heavenly Father. Once we do, he sinks his teeth in with accusations galore, bringing shame and regret. Every Christian should always have these two foundational facts in their mind:

- First, I am a sinner. I am lost, and my sin is so great that only Christ's death can save me. I cannot rely on my own willpower to overcome temptation. Only God's grace can save me.
- Second, I am absolutely loved. I am completely accepted. He sees me in Jesus Christ.

These two truths silence temptation. When I truly grasp the first truth, that I am a sinner, I become deeply aware that I need God's grace and power to stand against temptation. I know that Jesus laid down His life for me so that I would not give in to temptation. And when I fully comprehend the second truth, that I am entirely accepted in Jesus Christ, I remember that my identity rests not in my strength but in His. That confidence quiets every accusation before it can take hold. When I live out the gospel, Satan's strategies of temptation and accusation lose their grip and begin to crumble because they have been exposed as powerless lies.[13]

This battle for our minds is serious. We can no longer grant Satan *carte blanche* to our thoughts. We know he is after them. Our mind is the front line of this spiritual war between the kingdom of God and the kingdom of darkness. Our thoughts are where the active fighting is taking place. Knowing and being prepared for the tricks and deceptions of our enemy is of paramount importance. We can't allow our thoughts to grow these poisonous berries! Let's stop putting out the welcome mat to invite Satan in. No more foothold for him. We know his tricks, and we will protect our minds, question our berries, and get to the root. We know that Satan is looking for ways to sway us to consider that we can't trust God. He wants us to call God a liar.

Listening for Truth

1. Name a time when you have questioned God's character.
2. Consider what schemes the devil might be using in your mind. How have you possibly put out a welcome mat and invited him into your mind?
3. Now that you are aware of Satan's two strategies, how will you use the gospel to respond next time you are tempted or feel accused?
4. As you think about any berries growing on your Berry Bush, consider how they might be giving the devil an opening to influence your thoughts.

Chapter 9

SATAN WANTS YOU TO CALL GOD A LIAR

It was bedtime, and I was standing at the bathroom sink, coaxing our little daughter to climb onto the step stool so she could reach her toothbrush. She looked in the mirror and gazed affectionately at herself. "I am so beautiful!" she announced. With true contentment on her face, she looked in the mirror and really appreciated what she saw. "Ahh, childish innocence," I murmured to myself, but then I gulped as the thought hit me, "Why can't I say that when I look in the mirror?" I can't remember a time when I wasn't critical about myself, a time when I looked at my reflection and wasn't fighting off a feeling of not being enough, of not being worthy of love, or ashamed. Looking at my sweet little girl, I cringed, realizing that very soon she would no longer look in the mirror and hear the truth—that she is beautiful. This broken world will infect her heart. The everyday realities of living in a world of shattered shalom will shadow her thinking. She will begin to listen to the lies. Her thoughts, feelings, and emotions will reinforce the wrong belief, leaving her stuck in a rut. The significance of this groove will lead her to feel disconnected from God. The "I lies" she takes on—I am not enough, I am not lovable, I am stupid, I am ugly, I am useless, I am not worthy—are not the real lies she will believe. That bigger, more calculated, consequential lie is lurking underneath them all, attacking the character of God. We think that we simply need to replace our "I lies" with the truth about ourselves, but that will not get rid of them. They will remain and continue to damage our thinking and disconnect us from God. When we name the lies we believe about ourselves, we have not reached the root lie, because it goes deeper. It reaches all the way to the core of who we are, our identity. We are image bearers, made by God for God. When we entertain these lies, we are joining in with Satan in attacking the character of God.

My "I Lies" Really are "God Lies"

The next morning, as I was getting ready for the day, I looked in the mirror at myself, and I did not sound anything like my little daughter. Instead, I listened to the "I lies." Here is a peek into the conversation that I had with myself as I tried to Berry Bush my lie:

> Me: "Ugh! Look at me! I'm not enough—not pretty enough, not smart enough, not 'with it' enough."
>
> Inner Voice: Why am I feeling like this?
>
> Me: "Just look at me! I'm a mess. I do not have what others have."
>
> Inner Voice: Why do I think that?

Me: "When I compare myself to others, I can see the difference—I have huge deficits."

Inner Voice: Compare myself? Why am I comparing?

Me: "I know, I know, don't compare myself to others, but phew . . . I can see myself. It's evident."

Inner Voice: Why am I looking at myself—the way I see myself—from my perspective?

Me: "Well, I'm not taking into account God's perspective. These "I lies" are leading me to think that I need something else, or I just need to learn to love myself and accept myself. But, as I consider where these thoughts are leading, I realize that in actuality, I am choosing not to listen to God."

Inner Voice: Why?

Me: "I think He made a mistake! I know what the Bible says about me, but I don't believe that He truly deeply loves me and made me in His image."

Look! I found my root lie, and it is not about me. It is not an "I lie." It is a "God lie." By attacking the core of who I am, Satan has done it. He has gotten me to believe a lie about my identity. He has derailed me from the security of knowing who I am and whose I am. Now, I am in a rut, thinking these lies about myself, feeling not enough, behaving as if I need something else or need to be someone else. Ultimately, this rut has got me believing that I cannot trust God because He is a liar.

Looking back to Genesis and thinking through Eve's choice to believe a lie, it seems as if she has an "I lie" problem. She wants to be like God, and the lie that this fruit will make that happen snares her. However, it is not an "I lie." She isn't believing a lie about herself. As Jackie Hill Perry puts it:

> It's not because she forgot who she was. She didn't sin because she wasn't looking at herself, or because she didn't know herself, or because she had low self-esteem. If anything, she had way too much esteem. She sinned against God because she stopped believing the truth of who God was.[1]

Eve fell for a "God lie."

Made By God, For God

While I prepared breakfast, I turned on a sermon by Rechab Gray, pastor of New Creation Fellowship in Orlando, Florida. As I stirred the oatmeal, I heard him quote Herm Edwards from a time when he was coach of the New York Jets. Edwards was disgusted with players who were not giving 100 percent to win the game and felt compelled to remind them of the reason they played the game—their "why." Edwards shared this seemingly simple idea at a press conference. "You play to win the game. Hello? You play to win the game!"[2] As a follower of Jesus Christ, Rechab Gray admonished me, "You live to glorify God. Hello? You live to glorify God!"[3]

I stopped stirring. Of course! What was I doing letting those "I lies" linger in my mind? They had caused me to forget Isaiah 43:7, "*I have made them for my glory. It was I who created them*" (NLT). We were made by God, for God. That is our purpose statement. That is our "why." We live to exalt the name of Jesus Christ. When we listen to "I lies," we are not just denying our identity; we are defaming the character of God. Entertaining "I lies" clears the path for me to believe the lie underneath and ultimately call God a liar.

Who Told You?

One of my kids has been dealing with a girl in his class at school who has been hurting his feelings. Recently, almost daily, our child comes home with another example of the unkind words this girl has spewed at him. As we have talked it over, he shared his perspective. It amazes me. I wish that I could have this viewpoint. He explained, "I just consider where these words are coming from. I say to myself, 'Who told me that?' and it helps me to figure out who I should be listening to. I shouldn't listen to her."

After Adam and Eve ate the forbidden fruit, they hid from God, but He sought them out. Even though He knew everything about what had happened, He gave them a chance to share by asking: "*Where are you*" (Genesis 3:9)? "*Who told you were naked*" (3:11)? "*What is this you have done*" (3:13)? He gave them the opportunity to answer: Who told you these lies about yourself, about me? Who told you that I was untrustworthy? However, Adam and Eve played the blame game. Adam even blamed God, pointing out that he got the fruit from "*the woman whom* ***you*** *gave to be with me . . .* " (3:12 ESV emphasis mine). They were duped by the devil's lies. Those same lies that the Serpent told Eve are the ones he tells us. He continues to fool us with lies about who we are, what we need, and what we deserve, but underneath that lie is a lie about God. There is no such thing as "I lies" because all the lies we fall for will lead to a bigger lie at the root of it all. Satan's lies are a scheme to confuse us and cause us to forget that we are God's sons and daughters. The accuser does just that—accuses us, but God gives grace. When we, like the prodigal son, say "*I am no longer worthy to be called your son*" (Luke 15:21), the Father responds by stooping down to put sandals on our feet, a sign of dignity. He takes off his own robe and wraps it around us in total acceptance and belonging. On our finger, He places His signet ring, showing that we are His child. These "I lies" that we continue to perpetuate, thinking they are about us, are lies about Him.

As we blame ourselves, we have lost ourselves and forgotten who we are. As G. K. Chesterton wrote in his work *Orthodoxy*, "Every man has forgotten who he is. . . . We have all forgotten our names."[4] The other day I was listening to a podcast[5] and heard Hosanna Wong share about the rejection and depression she was going through when she created the spoken word called, "I Have a New Name."[6] I listened and worshiped as I breathed in the truth she spoke. God calls me *friend* (John 15:15), *chosen* (1 Thessalonians 1:4), *His masterpiece* (Ephesians 2:10), *His child* (Galatians 3:26), *greatly loved* (Romans 5:8), and *free indeed* (John 8:36). Just as He asked Adam and Eve, He asks us, "Who told you?" He offers an invitation to us to see the serpent's lies for what they are and choose instead to believe Him and His character. He is calling us by our "New Name." Will you call God a liar? How will you answer?

Listening for Truth

1. What do you see when you look in the mirror?
2. Do you have any "I lies" that you have tried to replace? How has it worked for you?
3. As you read through the names that Hannah Wong shared, which one resonates with you the most? Why?
4. As you think about the berries you have growing on your Berry Bush, are any of them "I lies"? Dig down through your feeder roots to find the "God lie" underneath.

PART III

YOUR ANXIETY ACTION PLAN

Chapter 10

ANXIETY IS COMING, IT'S TIME TO MAKE A PLAN

I had jury duty, and it took some finagling to figure out how to get four kids to three different schools and myself off in time to be at the downtown courthouse by seven thirty. Once I had everyone awake, I felt that familiar nausea come over me. I know it well. Anxiety has plagued me as far back as I can remember. Fear of doing new things and not feeling a sense of control are the biggest berries on my Berry Bush. To me, it seemed I had legitimate reasons to be anxious. I had never been to the courthouse, and it was downtown. Could I find the parking garage? Could I find a spot to park our ginormous Chevy Suburban? I had lost the letter with my juror number and instructions. Would that be a problem? Ugh! I felt sick. The heaviness encompassed me, and I felt drained of energy.

My son and I got in the car and headed down the freeway. Struggling to see, I turned on the defrost in vain. There was dense fog outside, and inside as well, because my head felt like it was filled with a misty haze. It was cold for Florida; I dropped my son off at school before the doors were even open and drove downtown. I felt queasy, and I was angry at myself. "Just because this is a new thing for you doesn't mean that you need to get stressed and anxious about it," I told myself. This anxiety is temporary, but it is common, and benign as it is, I feel it deeply. Above all, when I am anxious, I feel all alone. One thing that helped me that morning (and has helped me ever since I heard this teaching about it) was to take a YHWH breath. "In Hebrew, the name of God is Yahweh. It was considered too sacred to say out loud, so the vowels were removed. All that's left are consonants: YHWH. According to some scholars, YHWH is the sound of breathing."[1] I take a deep breath in and out. I listen for the name of my Maker. His name is on my lips. His breath is inside me. He is with me. I am not alone. I do not have to feel anxious. He is in control.

It seems as if the whole world is experiencing record amounts of anxiety. From our very young to senior citizens, worry and anxiety do not discriminate. All of us are susceptible. This book addresses anxiety as part of our belief system that goes down deep to a root lie about God that we are believing. That lie is underneath our anxieties, and the ruts that form keep us from truly experiencing God's love and care for us. However, I want to recognize that some of us do suffer from diagnosed debilitating anxiety disorders. I have witnessed the use of medications in treating anxiety disorders (and other mental health issues) as a lifeline that allows someone dealing with an anxiety disorder to function and helps them connect with God and others. I have a friend and coworker who has dealt with an anxiety disorder since she was a little girl. She worked on getting to the root of her lies by creating a Berry Bush and a Truth Tree. Recognizing the root lie of her berries has helped her. Working through the process of getting down to those roots with others has encouraged her.

Still, her diagnosis stands, and she continues to take her medication. Although this book will not be the cure to end all anxiety everywhere for everyone, my hope is that it will expose any lies we are believing about God's character and open our eyes to those moments when we are listening to those lies so that we can quickly call them out and live out the truth: He is our good, loving Father who is trustworthy. He cares for us and is in control of all things.

He made us. He knows everything about us, especially our tendency to be anxious. Phrases like "*Do not be anxious,*" "*Do not fear,*" and "*Do not worry*" appear many times in the Bible. It has been said that God put around 365 such commands in the Bible to remind us every day. One example is in Philippians 4:6. This challenge—"*do not be anxious about anything*"—seems impossible. The word *anxious* comes from the Greek verb *merimnao,* which denotes to divide or to distract. In Latin, *anxius* means choking or strangling.[2] That is exactly what anxiety does—it distracts us from the truth and then grabs us by the throat and squeezes. It chokes God out of our mind and leaves us suffocated with fear. Living in this fallen world, we know that fear and anxiety are issues we all have to deal with to some degree. As I was reading through Philippians recently, I was amazed that before telling the church not to be anxious, Paul referred to his own experience with anxiety. In his concern for the Philippian church, Paul admits to the anxiety that he struggled with as he made the decision to send back to them Epaphroditus, who had been very sick. He says, "*Therefore, I am all the more eager to send him, so that when you see him again you may be glad and I may have less anxiety*" (Philippians 2:28). Knowing that the church would be filled with joy at seeing Epaphroditus again alleviated Paul's anxiety. Community offers us a chance to manage our anxiety by sharing our burdens and joys with each other. This is something we all confront, and when we face it with others, we ease our anxiety and advance together toward peace. The expectation is not that we will never be anxious. Curtis Chang, author of *The Anxiety Opportunity*, relays this idea so well:

> We should no more expect Christians to be free of anxiety than we should expect Christians to be free of colds, mosquito bites, flat tires, sadness, or mental distraction. Paul brings up anxiety in Philippians 4:6 precisely because he expects it to be a persistent problem for his audience.[3]

Because we recognize that anxiety will be coming, it makes sense to be proactive. We need to devise a plan. If we wait for its arrival and then react, it will take over and feed our underlying lie about God.

Plan of Action

I think there are four crucial action steps that you can take to prepare your mind for the predictable moments of anxiety that will surface. Let's create a plan of action so that you can take the initiative instead of waiting around for those fears to hit.

Notice Your Anxiety

The first action is to notice when you are anxious. Mindfulness is a buzzword right now. It is acknowledging your feelings, thoughts, and sensations. See if you can begin to become aware of when you start to feel anxious. You might not even realize that you are anxious, but there are signs. Others are noticing. Ask someone who cares about you, how they know when you are anxious? Often, we are the last to know when we are exhibiting anxiety, but "Anxiety is like poker" author Steve Cuss explains, "We give off tells and then others can see our anxiety before we can."[4] My children are the first to notice when I am anxious. Sadly, I must confess that many times when they approach me and ask what is wrong, I don't appreciate their concern and snap back at them in an ugly tone. Anxiety is contagious, and I can see it in their little faces. I have passed it on to them. I do not want to share it with others. Let's decide now that we will not participate in spreading anxiety by infecting others, nor will we allow ourselves to catch it from them. I confess that I am still growing in this. With the help of resources like *Managing Leadership Anxiety* by Steve Cuss,[5] I am becoming more aware of when I am guilty of sharing my anxiety and tempted to catch it from others. The realization that I do not need to spread my anxiety to feel better about myself, nor do I need to react to other people's anxiety, has changed the atmosphere in my home and workplace. Have you have heard the saying, "Be a thermostat, not a thermometer?" Let's set the temperature, not just react to the climate. Plan ahead and choose to be the thermostat. Let's pledge not to propagate anxiety nor catch it from each other.

Focus on Gratitude

The second point in the plan has to do with where we are focusing. We ought to pay attention to what we are giving our attention. In his book, *The Men We Need*, Brant Hansen explains:

> What we pay attention to is everything. We should note just how the word "pay" fits. Our attention is a limited thing, and we have to manage it like finances. When I'm "paying" attention to something, I'm buying a ticket so my brain can attend.[6]

What kind of tickets are we buying? Are we telling our brain to focus on those things that increase our anxiety? Purposefully stop and consider where you are paying attention. Make an adjustment and choose to practice gratitude instead. Research shows that giving thanks can be transformational. Recently, an article popped up in my newsfeed about how thoughts change our brains. I had heard how beneficial gratitude could be in fighting anxiety, but I didn't know why. This report explained, "When people consciously practice gratitude, they get a surge of rewarding neurotransmitters, like dopamine, and experience a general alerting and brightening of the mind."[7] When gratitude is expressed, the brain releases the feel-good hormone, which shifts the brain's focus toward positive experiences. Giving thanks reduces the stress response and produces a calmer state, increasing our sense of overall well-being. *The Little Book of Gratitude*, by Robert Emmons, reports a study that found not only that gratitude lessens stress, but also that it is virtually impossible to be grateful and anxious at the same time. Gratitude and anxiety cannot coexist in the brain at the same time.[8] Let's plan now not to give so much time and attention to our worries but intentionally shift our focus to thanksgiving. After all, that is what Philippians 4:6 states immediately after the "*Do not be anxious about anything*" part. Paul lays out the steps to the plan: prayer and giving thanks. He emphasizes an attitude of gratitude throughout our prayer. "*By prayer and petition* ***with thanksgiving*** *present your requests to God*" (emphasis mine). Focusing on what we are grateful for will help curb anxiety. Gratitude is worth paying attention to. Plan now for that moment when anxiety raises its ugly head and begins to grab hold of you. In that moment, tell anxiety that you have prepared for this, and instead of "paying" attention to it, choose to focus on thankfulness.

Invite Jesus into Your Anxiety

We all have inner thoughts that either ramp up our anxiety or calm us down. We need to bring this inner voice to Jesus. He wants us to know the state of our soul. In *Boundaries for Your Soul*, by Allison Cook and Kimberly Miller, this idea of welcoming God into our chaotic and critical inner self is explored. They tell us to listen to our pain and notice the cues.

> When conflicted emotions threaten to derail you, seize the opportunity to evaluate your internal boundaries. What thoughts and feelings need your time, attention, and redirection? These overwhelming parts of your soul present opportunities for your growth and healing. After all, internal conflict is growth trying to happen.[9]

That is why you are reading this book. You want to change. You want relief. You want to get past this anxiety.

Recently, our twelve-year-old son had debilitating anxiety come out of nowhere and settle hard on him, paralyzing him at school and making life so difficult. This morning, he asked me, "When will I grow out of this?" I wanted to laugh, but I ended up crying with him. This is hard! Growth is hard. I encouraged him to try to see this overwhelming feeling as an opportunity. This is something I learned from Curtis Chang in his book *The Anxiety Opportunity*. Chang points out that we have an ideal self that we want to promote, but then our Anxious Self appears. He urges us to accept our Anxious Self rather than feel contempt for it. He brings this perspective:

> Our inner anxiety is a key context for our spiritual growth because Jesus meets us 'in there,' with our Anxious Self. If

> we reject our Anxious Self, we are rejecting the presence of Jesus. We are turning away from the place where He wishes to meet us. In a real sense, accepting Jesus requires accepting our Anxious Self.[10]

Chang reminds us that our Anxious Self is a part of us, and there is no way to shut it out. It won't go away and will "always figure out a way to be acknowledged. . . . We have to figure out how to get to acceptance"[11] Let's take Chang's sage advice and welcome in anxiety, seeing it as an opportunity to draw closer to Jesus.

Writing this book is part of my own process of accepting my Anxious Self. I have wrestled with it my whole life, and I can see how my children struggle with it too. One of our sons, Ben, has been held captive by it for many years. He spent a long time running from it, ashamed of it, scorning himself because of it, and even despising its presence in his life. Just last night, as I dropped him off at his dorm at college, he and I sat in the car, lingering for a few more minutes before I had to say goodbye. We talked about our anxiety. I told him how remorseful I was for the ways that, as his mother, I hadn't addressed his anxiety better. I shared how full of sorrow I was that he had to walk such a difficult path, but he wasn't sad. He shared that he was grateful for it because it had forced him to depend on God in a way that he never would have done otherwise. He saw it as something God has used to strengthen his faith and draw him into a relationship of complete dependence. Ben said, "Mom, I wouldn't be the man I am today if I had not had this anxiety. It has led me straight to God's arms. I truly am grateful for it." Wow! That is something, something beautiful, and his words are balm to my heart. They remind me of a quote I read in *Hudson Taylor's Spiritual Secret*. Hudson Taylor, one of the most influential missionaries in history, spent over fifty years bringing the gospel to China. In the book, his powerful perspective on handling stress and pressure is shared in something he used to say: "It doesn't matter really, how great the pressure is. It only matters where the pressure lies. See that it never comes between you and the Lord, then the greater the pressure, the more it presses you to his breast."[12] Picture in your mind the image that Taylor is painting. Are your inner thoughts intensifying the anxiety? Don't allow those berries to be barriers and come between you and Jesus. Instead, invite Him into your painful, overwhelmed condition so that the pressure will press you closer to God's heart. It will not be the burdens of life that break us, but whether we let them come between our God and us.

Berry Bush Your Fears

The fourth action step is what this book is all about. I have been leading others through the Berry Bush/Truth Tree process for years now, and many of those who have found it helpful have turned the title into a verb. They "Berry Bush their fears." That's what they call the action of digging down to their root lie. To begin, let's start with the berry. Think of that fear, the one that makes you break into a sweat and, as hard as you try to control and rationalize, it won't go away. It's that nagging worry that you bring to God, but then you cannot stop taking it back again. You try to give it to Him, but very soon you find yourself fretting over it. Eventually, you realize that you never truly gave it to God because you still have it. Once more, you pray and visualize yourself placing it in His hands, but it is not long before it's back, occupying your mind and heart. This is your poisonous berry, that pestering thought that keeps recurring in your mind. In chapter 18, we will go through step-by-step instructions for you to create your Berry Bush, but for now, go ahead and begin thinking of any poisonous berries that are harassing you. By naming your berries, you are telling them that you have a plan. You acknowledge them and welcome them. You are going to seize the opportunity those berries provide to excavate the lie underneath and replace it with the truth about God's character. The plan you create will help you notice anxiety and choose not to pay attention to it. Instead, you will focus on thankfulness. As you follow your plan, your perspective will change as you begin viewing anxiety as an opportunity to draw close to the Lord. You know anxiety is coming, so plan ahead and be ready for it. Next, let's consider the only real way to be prepared for anxiety and fear. Jesus told us, "*pray so that you will not fall into temptation*" (Mark 14:38). This will be the most essential part of our anxiety action plan.

Listening for Truth

1. How are you at noticing when you are anxious? When have you been guilty of sharing your anxiety?
2. What is something that you wish you were not "paying" attention to? How does it affect your thoughts, feelings, and behavior?
3. Think through what your plan looks like for the anxiety that will come. Write down your action plan.
4. Identify the berries that are troubling you.

Chapter 11

PLAN TO PRAY SO THAT YOU WILL NOT FALL INTO TEMPTATION

There is only one way to prepare your mind for the anxiety that is coming: prayer. I know, I know. This sounds like a simple spiritual answer—"Just pray anxiety away!" But looking at the life of Jesus, we can see that this is the way that He prepared Himself for anxiety. We are given many examples of Him praying. Not only did Jesus live it out during his own times of prayer, but when his disciples asked him to teach them to pray, He modeled for them the Lord's Prayer. Have you tried to follow this pattern in your own prayer time? I recently realized I haven't been praying all the parts of this prayer. I do spend time praising our Father and asking for His kingdom to come. I plead with Him for His will to be done. I ask for our daily bread, beg for forgiveness, and consider how to forgive others. However, I have not paid much attention to the last two lines where Jesus instructs us that "*this is how you should pray. . . . Lead us not into temptation but deliver us from the evil one*" (Matthew 6:9, 13).

Why have I avoided these two lines? One reason is probably that the word *temptation* has confused me. In my mind, it brings a negative connotation with the idea of God tempting us by enticing us to do evil, but that is impossible because we know that James 1:13 says that God does not tempt or lure us into evil. Replacing *temptation* with other translations, such as "testing" or "trial," has helped me. Now I pray something like what Tim Mackie says on the Bible Project's podcast: "Father, I would rather not go through a test, but if You are going to lead me into a test, then please deliver me from the evil one."[1] What I am really asking is for God to give me discernment in those areas where I am most likely to fall into temptation and be lured away from Him.

Another reason I have overlooked these two lines and have not been praying for spiritual protection is that I put all my focus on the physical world, appearing blind to the reality of the spiritual realm. When anxiety and uncertainty of the future consume my thoughts, I prove true the advice of Screwtape in a letter to his demon nephew, Wormwood, in C. S. Lewis's book, *The Screwtape Letters,* "There is nothing like suspense and anxiety for barricading a human's mind against the Enemy. He wants men to be concerned with what they do; our business is to keep them thinking about what will happen to them."[2] Those berries on my Berry Bush have barricaded my mind against the Lord. They prohibit me from a real relationship with Him and cause me to forget that I have an enemy who does not want God's name to be honored, and does not want me to experience God's goodness or forgiveness. This accuser seeks to keep us discouraged and distracted. His plan is for us to feel overwhelmed with fear and full of insecurity. Cunningly, he works to keep us oblivious to the real battle that is going on. However, Jesus reminds us with these last two lines of His prayer that we need God to stand against our enemy. When we pray "*lead us not into temptation,*" we recognize that we are weak. We ask Him to guide us away from situations that might tempt us to sin. We admit we are vulnerable and need His protection, because we know we can't do it on our own. We are to actively be praying against those things that steer us off course. I should be earnestly praying for Him to lead me away from the things that could easily entice me away from Him and deliver me at all times from the work of the evil one. Through this prayer, we confess that we have no clue how to face the day or what it will bring, but we know that we need protection from the devil's attacks. We know that we need to pray.

Jesus's Anxious Prayer in the Garden

During the heaviest moment of anxiety for Jesus, He depended on prayer. The Gospels tell us that the night before his crucifixion, He took his disciples and went to a quiet orchard full of olive trees to pray. He had just celebrated the Last Supper with His friends, told them of His coming death, and even showed them using the symbols of bread and wine. He predicted their denial. He knew they would desert him, telling them that on this very night they would all fall away. Now, He leads them out to the portion of the garden called the "Oil Press." This night that Jesus spends in prayer is a defining moment for Him and for all of us who follow Him. Because through His wrestling with His emotions and the process of working through His thoughts, He shows us how to pray through anxiety. In Mark 14:33, we are told that as they walked, He "*began to be deeply distressed and troubled.*" He dreaded the agony that was coming. In that moment, He chose to pray and ask others to pray with Him. He took His closest disciples with Him and described to them what He was feeling by saying, "*My soul is overwhelmed with sorrow to the point of death*" (Matthew 26:38).

I know that Jesus understands our struggles with temptation, pain, and suffering, and I am familiar with verses like Hebrews 4:15, which says, "*For we do not have a high priest who is unable to empathize with our weaknesses, but we have one who has been tempted in every way, just as we are—yet he did not sin.*" But when I see Jesus in this moment, I see how He faced overwhelming emotions. This realization makes His empathy seem tangible and real to me in my own moments of feeling "*overwhelmed with sorrow.*" In those moments, I don't even know what to say. I do not have words. That must have been how Jesus felt too because His words reflect the disturbed, agitated soul described in Psalms 6, 88, and 42. As we hear His words and observe His actions, it almost seems that, as Tim Mackie describes, He is experiencing a "panic attack."[3]

He was filled with anguish, agitated, and overwhelmed. He asked His three closest friends to stay with Him, keep watch, and pray. He went a little farther away from them and fell with his face to the ground, His body buckling under the crushing grief. He cried out, "*Abba, Father, everything is possible for you. Please take this cup of suffering away from me. Yet I want your will to be done, not mine*" (Mark 14:36 NLT). In this dark moment, Jesus is in agony as the overwhelming emotions descend, and He tries to navigate through them using the words of the prayer that He taught His disciples to pray. "*Your will be done.*" This was a prayer that He must have prayed many times as He sought the Father's guidance throughout the years.

"*Your will be done*" were the words that began to steady His soul as Jesus reckons with not wanting to drink the cup. It was not just the idea of being tortured to death that Jesus didn't want to go through. It was drinking from **that** cup. It was becoming sin for you and me. It meant being forsaken by the Father. The time had come for Him to drink the cup of God's wrath for everyone. He would take on the sins of all of us—the whole world (1 John 2:2). "*For God made Christ, who never sinned, to be the offering for our sin, so that we could be made right with God through Christ*" (2 Corinthians 5:21 NLT). The thought of taking this cup led Jesus to ask His Father if there was any other way for the sin of mankind to be covered. Would His Father pursue a different plan for the price of sin, one that would not involve having Jesus take this cup and become sin?[4] He shows us that in prayer, we can express our true feelings. As He exposed His dread of the terrible cup and His wish that He did not have to drink it, Jesus also affirmed His commitment to His Father's will.

Then, He went back to His friends and found them asleep. We can hear His voice pleading with them as He asks, "*Couldn't you watch with me even one hour*" (Matthew 26:40). Having already warned Peter of his impending betrayal, He addressed him, "*Keep watch and pray, so that you will not give in to temptation. For the spirit is willing, but the body is weak*" (Matthew 26:40–41 NLT)! He gave them the "why," explaining, "*Pray so that you will not fall into temptation.*" This is straight from the prayer that He had taught them, "*Lead us not into temptation, but deliver us from the evil one*" (Matthew 6:13). It is the middle of the night, and they are tired. He doesn't condemn them but reminds them that, although they have the sincere desire to do as He asked, as humans, they are frail and weak. Ultimately, their "flesh" decides for them unless, through prayer, they rely on God's strength.

This is the choice He is presenting to them: a mindset, a way of thinking. Remember that "*the spirit is willing, but the flesh is weak*" (Matthew 26:41). My walk with Christ has proved this warning true. Paul explains it in Romans 7:15 "*What I want to do I do not do, but what I hate I do.*" With this statement, "*the spirit is willing, but the body is weak*!" (Matthew 26:41 NLT) Jesus defines what it is like to follow Him. Here, He is clarifying that prayer is the only answer to combat the weakness of the body. Prayer is the plan for those moments of stress, temptation, and anxiety. Jesus warns us to be aware that temptation is on its way, especially when we are vulnerable. Alone, we cannot resist. God's strength is our defense, and that is why prayer is essential.

Second Time

He left them a second time and returned to pray. He prayed the same prayer, but take note of the difference. There is a slight change. Tim Mackie explains, "Before, His request came across a little like my prayers sound, 'If it is possible, please take the cup away from me. I don't want it. Yet, not what I want but what you want—but here is what I want.'"[5] Now, the second time He asks, "*My Father! If this cup cannot be taken away unless I drink it, your will be done*" (Matthew 26:42 NLT). Jesus has moved forward, toward the Father's plan, and it is as if He is saying, "It is not possible for me to avoid this, is it? OK then, may Your will be done." He is reckoning with His emotions as He comes face to face with His calling of total separation from God so that He can pay for all sin. He walks back over to His disciples and finds them asleep. Their explanation was that "*their eyes were heavy*" (Matthew 26:43). Another example of our willing spirit, but weak flesh.

Third Time

So, He left them for the third time and went back about a stone's throw away to pray the same prayer. His suffering was so great that in anguish, He prayed more earnestly (Luke 22:44). He persisted in prayer. Sometimes, when we are in agony, that is the last thing we do. We go to the Lord for peace, but don't find it. That is when we should go back, but instead we give up and look for other ways to soothe ourselves. We tried prayer. Now, we think, let's try ice cream, Netflix, alcohol, among other things. Jesus persevered in prayer. Because He kept going back in prayer, the last time He returned to the disciples, He was changed. He had peace that wasn't there in the beginning. He didn't get the answer that He originally prayed for, but He had peace. He was calm, resolute, and determined as Judas approached Him to greet Him with a kiss. Ray Pritchard puts into words the impact of Christ's decision that night to pray:

> The victory of Calvary was won on Thursday night. The battle was won before Judas ever planted his betrayer's kiss. The battle was won before a spike was ever nailed in the hands of Jesus. The battle was won when he prayed. He did not fail in his testing because he did not fail in his praying.[6]

"Will you pray for me?" Ben calls me from college and asks. As I shared earlier, anxiety is a part of Ben's life. It has plagued him since he was young, but instead of turning him away from God, this angst turns him toward his Savior. I ask how I should pray, and he answers like he always does, "Pray that I will trust God." We have gone through the Berry Bush together, and he knows that one of his root lies is that God cannot be trusted. Fear tries to asphyxiate his faith, but he reaches out and grabs my hand. I begin, my voice cracks and sounds too loud as I wrestle with my own emotions of "Why? Why won't this anxiety leave? God, how do we reach Your peace?" In the beginning, instinctively, I wanted to demand that God do something to fix the fear, but now I realize that this is a journey that he and God are walking together. For a long time, we have been praying with him during this anxiety tour of duty. Prayer is a vital part of the anxiety action plan that my husband and I have made with our child, but I can also see that it truly is God's plan. This time of testing has caused him to have a deep dependence on the Lord, and it has drawn us closer to each other. As time has gone on, we can both see how God is using his fear to pull him into a more intimate relationship with the Lord Himself. Without the expectation of anxiety and our plan to be prepared for it, Ben's fears would have taken over and fed his underlying lie about God. He has done the work to figure out his berries and dug down deep to discover and excavate his root lie. The ugly lie underneath is that God is not trustworthy. Today, he focuses on the root truth that God is trustworthy and reminds himself of who God really is—faithful and true. Because Ben knows where those berries and ugly root originated, he understands what the lie underneath is all about. It's all about God. It is God's character that is under attack.

Listening for Truth

1. Considering how Jesus warned His disciples to pray so that they wouldn't fall into temptation, how will your prayer life reflect the last two lines of the Lord's Prayer?
2. Reflect on how much Jesus stressed the importance of prayer and the reason He gave for it. How can you respond?
3. Are your berries driving you to pray or keeping you from praying? Explain their impact on your prayer life.
4. Describe a time when your berries acted as barriers and "barricaded" your mind and kept you from complete communion with God.

Chapter 12

PLAN TO BE CONFRONTED WITH LIES ABOUT GOD'S CHARACTER

"Hmmm" was all the doctor said as she stared at the file in front of her. We sat in uneasy silence for a while as I held my little eighteen-month-old daughter, fear gripping me as I pulled her in closer to me. I knew something was wrong even before the doctor confirmed it. I had noticed that she wasn't meeting her milestones and that she wasn't gaining weight. It was like she had just stopped. Why? I swallowed hard, thinking of all the mistakes I had made as a mother. What had I done? What had I missed? This conversation with the doctor led to more doctors as we began a journey of discovery to find out why she had stopped growing and what to do about it.

Throughout those months, I lived in fear, both hopeful and hesitant, wanting to know the answer but dreading to find out. I was struggling to believe that God was working out all things for the good of those who love Him (Romans 8:28), wrestling with verses that speak of God's goodness. I was a missionary. I should be speaking of God's faithfulness, but I did not display a heart of faith. I lived in constant anxiety and alarm. I can look back now, twelve years later, and it seems like a bad dream, but I still remember how it felt. The runaway emotions of angst and despair were engulfing me day and night. It was all I could think of. There was hopelessness due to the lack of answers from the medical community. Fear and everything that comes with that wrapped itself around me like a tight and suffocating rope.

Months into her treatment, the situation began to look more positive. On a gray, overcast day, I sat on our bed reflecting on a devotion that a coworker had shared. It was a well-known story of the time when Jesus fell asleep in the boat, and the disciples woke Him, asking Him to help because of a terrible storm. He got up, calmed the wind and waves, and then asked them, "*Why are you so afraid? Do you still have no faith*" (Mark 4:40)? They were overwhelmed with fear and said to each other, "*Who is this? Even the wind and the waves obey him*" (Mark 4:41)! As I considered these verses, I had to ask myself, "Who is this God I am praying to? How does my understanding of who He is impact how I respond when I am afraid? I was right there with the disciples, shaking Jesus awake, frustrated at Him, and scared. But then He spoke; everything calmed, and I realized some things. It was His idea to get into the boat in the first place. He could have told the wind and waves to be calm before they started, or not even gone out on the boat. Instead, He put them in this situation and asked them not to respond naturally, but to respond with faith. He allowed that opportunity for the disciples to see what fear really is. When He rebuked them asking, "*Why are you so afraid?*" He called out fear and defined it for them and for us. Fear is the opposite of faith. Knowing that definition changes my whole perspective on my own stormy boat trip with Jesus, His head on a pillow and sound asleep in the stern. Here is the question: Can I lie down beside Him and rest my head on the pillow too?

Fear Is the Opposite of Faith

As believers in our Lord Jesus Christ, we want to live lives of faith, not lives of fear. We know in our heads and declare with our lips that Jesus is the Lord of all. We proclaim verses like these:

- "*The Lord is my light and my salvation—Whom shall I fear*" (Psalm 27:1)?
- "*For God has not given us a Spirit of fearfulness, but one of power, love, and sound judgment*" (2 Timothy 1:7 HCSB).
- "*For you did not receive the spirit of slavery to fall back into fear, but you received the Spirit of adoption, by whom we cry out, 'Abba, Father'*" (Romans 8:15 ESV)!

As Christians, we say we believe these verses, but when we look at how we live our lives, we realize there is a gap. Author Steve Cuss has labeled this the "expectation gap,"[1] a gap between what we believe about God versus what we experience from God. If we were honest, those of us who want so much to live for Jesus would look at our beliefs in Him, look at the way we live our lives, and acknowledge that there is a gap. Cuss proposes that we have a gap between our cognitive beliefs, what we think about Jesus, and our body beliefs, the way we experience life.[2] I know this is evident in my life because knowing these verses is one thing, but living them out is another. Reality shows us to be fearful people, spending anxious hours fretting and worrying. Every morning, I look in the mirror, and I see that worry crease in my forehead getting deeper with each passing day. All that worry cannot change anything. As Corrie Ten Boom put it, "Worry is like a rocking chair. It keeps you busy but cannot bring you farther."[3] I come from a long line of worriers. It's in my DNA. Like a scout badge, my family wears the sash of worry and takes pride in earning the Worry Merit Badge. My grandmother used to tell me, "Well, at least I feel like I am doing something when I worry."

The Worry Backpack

The other day, I was reminded how futile worry is while taking my five-year-old daughter to the park. As we prepared to leave the house, she said she would take a few toys with her. I didn't pay much attention and filled some water bottles for us to take along. As we walked down the sidewalk to the park, I noticed that she was carrying a large, cumbersome backpack. I wondered what in the world she had thought so necessary to bring along. It didn't take long for her little body to give way to the heaviness of the bag, and she asked for Mommy's help. As I took it from her, I was amazed she had carried it that far; it was very heavy. We made it to the park, and she ran off to play with a friend. I was curious to see what was in the heavy bag, so I unzipped the backpack to find out. It was full of rocks! She explained later that she wanted to carry a big backpack like her big brothers wear for school and decided rocks would be the best thing because they are big and heavy. This reminded me of my experience with worry. Fretting about things like circumstances, finances, and kids' health are rocks that I put in my daily backpack, usually one after the other, and yet, they are of no use. Carrying it around doesn't do anything but hurt my back!

Jesus asks us in Matthew 6:27, "*Can any of you by worrying add a single hour to your life?*" Obviously not. We all know that Jesus has told us not to worry, but we still do it. Why? If you find yourself carrying around a backpack of rocks, ask yourself, "Why?" Decide to take worry seriously and treat it for what it is: a lie. Do not excuse yourself and make light of it. Treat it like the poisonous berry that it is. Start digging to get to the root of why you are allowing yourself to worry.

In her book *One Thousand Gifts*, author Ann Voskamp proposed that refusing to trust and choosing to stress should be called "practical atheism."[4] When we worry, we act as if God is not in control, like He is not the creator of the universe and all there is. We act as if we do not believe all things will work together for good. When we live out a fearful life, we show everyone around us that God is not reliable. He is not trustworthy. And that we truly do not believe.

Just as the psalmist expressed a longing for the whole world to know what God is like, I want God's name to be made famous: "*May your ways be known throughout the earth, your saving power among people everywhere*" (Psalm 67:2 NLT). I do not want my life to spread lies about God's reputation. If I genuinely do believe that God is who He says He is, then I need to get serious and acknowledge what worry really is—a lie about the character of God.

Our Response in Affliction Testifies to the Character of God

It was 2010, and I was sitting in a conference in downtown Indianapolis surrounded by over 6,000 women when I heard a teaching from Joni Eareckson Tada. She totally opened my eyes to how my response to hardship can teach the angelic beings about God's character. If you've been a Christian for any length of time, you probably know Joni's story. She has been a quadriplegic since 1967. Living more than five decades now in a wheelchair, enduring chronic pain, and surviving breast cancer, she knows suffering. Throughout all this, she glorifies God and points others to worship Him despite difficult situations. That evening she was speaking on Ephesians 3:9–10 (GNT), describing this good news:

> *God, who is the Creator of all things, kept his secret hidden through all the past ages, in order that at the present time, by means of the church, the angelic rulers and powers in the heavenly world might learn of his wisdom in all its different forms.*

Joni explained that:

> God will use our lives as a blackboard upon which He chalks marvelous lessons about Himself for the benefit of millions and millions of unseen beings, angels and even demons . . . they are intensely interested in the way I respond to my affliction because it teaches them something about God.[5]

I had only seen suffering from my perspective, as something that is happening to me. Sure, I knew that my friends and neighbors were watching, but I had never considered the perspective of the spiritual realm. I should have because the Bible shows us how Satan comes to the Lord and is permitted to test Job. He hoped to prove that Job didn't really love God. Satan wanted to show that Job only loved God because of His blessings. At first, he attacked all Job's possessions and loved ones, but Job still praised God. Satan went back to God and asked permission to attack Job's body, thinking physical pain would be the way to get Job to curse God, but that didn't work either. For his third attempt, Satan used Job's friends to share distortions of the truth about God's character. In his subtle and deceptive way, Satan attempted to convince Job that God was vengeful and severe. It was an all-out character assassination not just for Job's ears, but also those in the spirit world. Job's friend Eliphaz accused him of deserving everything from God because of his wickedness. He stated that God doesn't trust any of His creatures and specifically points out, "*Even in his servants he puts no trust, and his angels he charges with error*" (Job 4:18 ESV). This comment and others like it (15:15) are obviously intended to warp the character of God in the angels' minds and cause them to ponder the lies that God doesn't care about you, God is not trustworthy, God is not good. Despite all Satan's attempts to dissuade him, Job would not back down. His response to all his afflictions revealed that God is worth following. His life and mind were a battlefield where the mightiest forces of the universe converged in all-out war, fighting over God's character.

Now that we are aware that we are engaged in cosmic warfare, we cannot give in! Even when we are immersed in suffering, though our emotions tell us to doubt and to fear, we will not because we do not want to defame God's name. When we pray and beg the Lord to see us through, He sustains us, and the angels and demons learn something about God's mercy. When we face hardship, we are never isolated. While wrestling with loneliness and the pull of depression, Joni recognized the familiar lie that she was unseen and uncared for—and in that moment, she decided:

> I dare not let myself go down that dark grim path because the stakes are too high. God's reputation is on the line. My life is on display and so is yours and it's all for God's glory. When

> the spirit world sees God's strong arms uphold you in your weakness, the Father gets the glory. When the spirit world sees God come to your aid when you are fearful, the Father gets the glory. The angelic and dark powers of the entire universe . . . are amazed to see that it is the mighty strength of Christ's resurrection that is giving you the power to say no to bitterness and yes to grace. . . . In short, the spirit world watches your perseverance under pressure and thinks Whoa! How great her God must be to inspire such loyalty through such suffering. This is what it means to glorify God in your afflictions.[6]

No matter what is going on in our lives, we can trust that God is right in the thick of it with us. Knowing that His reputation is at stake through my response in affliction reconfigures how I choose to respond. My action plan prepares me to recognize that the real issue with my berries is God's reputation. No longer will I spread lies about His character with my doubt and self-focus. From now on, I will fix my eyes on His grace and goodness, but to do that, first I need to dig down to my lie underneath.

Listening for Truth

1. Take a moment and consider how your back feels. What rocks (aka poisonous berries) are you carrying in your worry backpack?
2. What would your life (i.e., your thoughts, feelings, behavior) look like if you took worry seriously and treated it like the lie that it is?
3. Knowing that your perseverance in suffering is a part of this cosmic war, how will you plan to respond?
4. The real issue with our berries is God's reputation and the lies about His character that we spread through them. How do you plan to address your berries?

PART IV

THE BERRY BUSH

Chapter 13

THE ROOT LIE: GOD IS NOT GOOD

As I sat in the emergency room cubicle separated only by curtains, I listened to the people crying out on both sides of me. Different voices were pleading, "Oh, God!" "God help me! God please!" All kinds of whispers and groans called out to God, asking for His intervention in their pain. I was there with my sister. I was nineteen years old, and she was twenty-four. We were doing the same—praying to God for her healing. I doubted that these people who were crying out to God on the other side of the curtain even knew Him, really, or whether their cry was just an exclamation, something the soul cries out when we are overcome with pain and despair. But my sister and I were different. We were genuinely close with God. We had an intimate relationship with Him. We had walked with Him since we were children. We had experienced His love and faithfulness. However, in my own youth and immaturity, I had never had a reason to question His goodness . . . until now. Why didn't God heal my sister? Knowing how much she loved Him and served Him, why would He allow her to be in pain? Why didn't He do what I asked Him to do? Why God?

Why don't You give me what I think is best? If You are good, why did You allow this to happen?

All of us must approach and answer this question sooner or later in life. It boils down to this fact: God doesn't do what we want Him to do. If He is good, why doesn't He do good in my life? If He is all-powerful and all-knowing, why won't He make it all better? This part of my faith journey took me a while. I turned away from God, not believing in His goodness. I was angry and grieving. It felt futile to continue in a relationship with Him. How can I trust that God is good when my circumstances are terrible? They held me in turmoil for so long. I wanted to believe that God was good, but everything around me in my life did not point to that.

Some time passed, and one Sunday in church, the worship group began singing "Blessed Be Your Name." [1] The lyrics are about praising God in all circumstances, both good and bad. "*The Lord gave me what I had, and the Lord has taken it away. Praise the name of the Lord*" (Job 1:21 NLT)! I could not sing it. I did not want to sing it. I knew they were the words of Job. I knew his story. But that did not matter to me. I did not want to tell my heart to choose to praise God when He would take things from me.

Gradually, the kindness of God kept drawing me to Him. I wanted to move closer to Him, but I kept myself guarded. I knew in my head that God was good, but I could not bring myself to truly embrace that truth. I would pray, asking Him to remove that distance between us, but then quickly I was right back there, pulling away. I knew that I must be believing a lie. Then one day, I took out a sheet of paper and sketched out a Berry Bush. I labeled my poisonous berry as the distant feeling between God and me. Then, I asked myself "why?" many times until I eventually got down to the root lie, God is not good. The conversation in my head went something like this:

> Inner voice: I wonder why I'm feeling so distant from God right now.
>
> Me: Could it be because I'm carrying hurt and anger? I feel like I am.
>
> Inner voice: Why? Where is that hurt and anger coming from?
>
> Me: I think it's because I believed God could have fixed everything.
>
> Inner voice: What makes me feel that way?
>
> Me: It seems like He ignored me. He knew I was hurting, but didn't step in to help my sister when I prayed.
>
> Inner voice: Why do I feel like that? How does that leave me feeling toward Him?
>
> Me: Like maybe He doesn't care when I suffer.
>
> Inner voice: And underneath that—Why do I feel like He doesn't care? What's the deeper fear?
>
> Me: It feels like God is not good; if He were, He would have healed my sister.

I found my root lie: God is not good. I went ahead and sketched out the Berry Bush. Here is my poisonous berry of pain, and the feeder roots that nourish my horrible root lie about God.

Figure 1. Berry Bush: God Is Not Good

If God Cared, He Would Do Something

Growing up at church almost every Sunday, the pastor would start out like this: "God is good!" The congregation would respond: "All the time." He would come back with "All the time," and then it was the congregation's turn to declare "God is good!" Looking back, it seemed easy to say. As a little girl, I meant it, but later when my sister was so sick, it was too hard to affirm God's goodness. I didn't want to. It has been thirty-one years since I first worked through my doubts about God's goodness, but this lie has reared its head many times since. After seeing how I was allowing my mind to get stuck in the rut of this lie, I chose to work to believe the truth that God is good. The effort of digging through my thoughts to recognize that they lead to my feelings, which in turn affect my behavior and reinforce what I believe, obliged me to call this lie out. The moment this lie first appears and I think, "That's not fair; if God cared, He would do something," I stop and speak the truth—God is good. He is good. As I say it, a broad assuredness settles over me. It's not my circumstances that I am referring to when I talk of God's goodness; it's just who He is.

In the example of having a distant feeling between God and me, I am not implying that every time we experience that feeling, the cause is a root lie that God is not good. It could be a time of trial in the desert for which the Lord has a purpose in your situation or some other reason. Look in the psalms for examples of times when that distant feeling is present. Psalm 13:1 asks, "*O Lord, how long will you forget me? Forever*" (NLT)? While the psalms often give voice to the feeling that God is distant in our suffering, they also consistently affirm an underlying trust in His ultimate power and love. I wanted to share my example because I thought that I had already dealt with my disappointment in God from years earlier, but I had not. I had held on to those feelings. The Berry Bush exercise helped me discover the cause of that distance.

Right now, I am writing this in the waiting room of a stroke rehab center. I watch patient after patient enter. I see them struggle to cross the threshold as parts of their bodies are unable to perform what was once so easy for them. I wonder if they have trouble believing in the goodness of God, considering how significantly a stroke has changed their lives. I am here because I drove my friend to her appointment. She isn't able to drive because during the birth of her second child, she suffered an amniotic fluid embolism.[2] She died six times, but miraculously was revived. She was placed on life support and spent nine days in a coma. Now, three years later, she is still working through her disability. Her life is so very hard! How can she declare that God is good? Our son's teacher is deep in despair as he and his wife grieve the loss of their stillborn baby. How can they continue to profess that God is good? A coworker is in hospice, his last days on earth as his body succumbs to cancer. How can his wife and children continue to sing of God's goodness? How do we live between these two realities—one of suffering in grief and the other of trusting in God's sovereignty? Sadly, it seems like there are only two options for us: blame God or run from the pain. We either accuse God of stacking the deck against us and think, "If this is who God is, I don't want any part of Him," or we ignore the pain, pushing it down. Either response leaves us hopeless, and the overwhelming feeling of grief remains. We feel horrible because we don't believe that, as a Christian, we should be feeling these emotions.

We tell ourselves we should live in hope and joy. We don't want to allow ourselves to recognize the reality of sadness. Author and counselor Christine Chappell explains that for many Christians when faced with grief their response is, "Well, this is a very negative feeling, emotion, and actually I shouldn't have it because I have hope in the Lord."[3] When we say this, we try to force ourselves to live out what we should believe, but we are not able to get through the sorrow. We focus on our own unrighteousness, and self takes center stage in our thoughts. Chappell explains that over the years she has recognized the necessity, even in the midst of her pain, to learn to "put Christ at the center of those experiences instead of myself at the center."[4] She has learned to lament, to lay out her complaint and ask for God's help saying, "Lord, I want to trust you with this. Help my unbelief." She confesses:

> Once I say amen after my lament, I don't feel any better usually. I'm still feeling this tension. The problem is unresolved. I've taken it to the Lord, but He hasn't immediately shaken a wand and changed anything. I have to live in this uncomfortable emotion for a period of time.[5]

What do I do when what I am experiencing does not line up with what I believe? How can my life be so hard and God be good? Can a good God allow evil? Author of *Dark Clouds Deep Mercies* Mark Vroegop answers that question, "God is good, and life is hard. In the Bible, they don't reconcile; they just are. The psalms of lament show us those two things actually coexist in the Christian faith."[6] The Bible has words and language that describe the pain we walk through. It shows us how to grieve with hope. Holding both of these at the same time is something the Lord helps us to learn. Vroegop defines lament as "a prayer in pain that leads to trust."[7] He points out, "One out of every three psalms are laments. God intended for us to have this language to talk to him when life really gets hard."[8]

Knowing that the ratio of laments is 1:3, he challenges us to have the expectation that one out of every three days in our life could be difficult or sorrowful days for us. "Lament is rooted in what we believe. It is a prayer loaded with theology. Christians affirm that the world is broken, God is powerful, and he will be faithful. Therefore, lament stands in the gap between pain and promise."[9] Every human has a "Theology of suffering,"[10] but Vroegop admonishes us as followers of Jesus to make certain that ours is biblical because walking through pain will test what we truly believe about God.

God Is Good – It Is Who He Is

On long road trips, when it's time to stop for gas, my family always gets excited to pull into Buc-ee's—a massive convenience store. It's packed with everything from unique merchandise and fun snacks to mouthwatering barbecue, tempting desserts, and famously clean bathrooms. Not long ago, I found myself standing in line for the women's restroom, holding my young daughter's hand. As we waited, we passed the time admiring the paintings and photographs hanging along the hallway walls, each one for sale. We played a little game, trying to pick our favorite. She pointed excitedly to an unusual painting of a cow, its playful, exaggerated face surrounded by swirls of pinks and purples. "That one's my favorite," she said. "I love the colors and the silly face. It looks like the cow is saying something!" Smiling, I asked, "I wonder what he could be saying?" Without missing a beat, she replied in her matter-of-fact way, "Mooo, of course!" I perused my options and quickly noticed a photograph of an expanse of a valley, surrounded by mountains and a cloudy sky. Yet there were rays of sunlight streaming through the clouds, shining down into the darkened valley. Although the valley seemed like a sad place, the hope and joy of light beams streaming through the thick clouds changed what could have been dark and scary into a hopeful scene. When I gazed at that valley scene, I saw God shining through, bringing His light, peace, strength, faithfulness, and assuredness of His presence even in the valley.

Valetta

That photo reminded me of my friend. She is a missionary with One Mission Society. Valetta knows about trusting in the goodness of God. Her journey with Jesus has taught her about His goodness. She is a beautiful picture of Christ—wise, kind, bold, and joyful. Whenever she introduces herself, she explains the significance of her unique name. In Italian, it means "valley," and fittingly, Valetta's life has been marked by seasons spent in life's lowest places. She has walked through the valley of the shadow of death not once, but three times. Yet, as she navigated through the darkest chapters of her life, she learned to view adversity from a higher vantage point—God's perspective—from the mountaintop rather than the depths of the valley. From that elevated view, she has come to recognize the beauty that exists even in the valley, and her life continues to reflect and proclaim the goodness of God. In her book, *Another Valley, Another Victory: Three Tragedies, One Faithful Woman, Victory in Jesus,*[11] she tells her story, the deeply painful account of how she lived through the valley of tragedy. She begins her book by describing the feeling that tragedy brings when it hits:

> I've tried many times to analyze the phenomenon of tragedy—how a single moment, a single event, a single word can forever alter the shape of one's world. The mind struggles to

> comprehend, yet it revolts. The heart will not accept what reason insists is fact. Then, slowly, at intervals, the facts began to seep down from the numbed brain into the heart, bringing a kind of paralysis. At the same time comes a vague, nagging sense of guilt. Why me? Why us? Are the questions that intrude, again and again. Where did we fail? Was there something we could have done that we didn't do? Is God punishing us?[12]

Valetta works through those questions as she recounts her deep valleys of sorrow. She met Henry the very first day of her senior year, and before she was out of her teens, after just one year of college, they knew they wanted to spend their lives together. It wasn't long before they welcomed a beautiful little blonde-haired son. They named him Danny. Henry and Valetta both loved serving the Lord, and Henry was eager to be a pastor. When the baby was just ten days old, they began leading a small church in Michigan.

Excitedly, they followed God's call, trusting that He would guide them. They worked hard to build up the church, and Valetta soon found out she was expecting again. Danny was a chubby baby with blue eyes and the delight of her life. He smiled at everyone and got plenty of attention in the small town. She describes him as having a "personality that would charm a cobra."[13] When Danny was two years old, he became very sick. When Valetta took him to the doctor, she was crushed to find out that Danny had acute leukemia and there was no cure at that time. She couldn't believe it. How could this happen? Through many tears, Valetta prayed to God, "If you made the world and created human beings. It would be nothing for you to heal Danny."[14] The church was praying fervently for his healing, but Valetta explains, "sometimes God heals and sometimes He doesn't."[15]

One morning, when she went to his crib, she found that he had passed away in the night. This was her first time through the valley.

Valetta and Henry picked up the pieces of their grief, and life continued with their newborn son, Leon. They moved from that country church, deciding that Henry would return to school, but a church in Kalamazoo approached him, asking him to come and serve their church. It was there that they welcomed a baby daughter named Lorna. Henry continued pastoring, and the church continued to grow. One day, Henry noticed a few enlarged lumps growing in his neck. It seemed unbelievable when the doctor told them that he had Hodgkin's Lymphoma. He was only twenty-six. About this time, a missionary visited them, and Henry felt challenged to consider a dream he had of being involved in missions. He asked the Lord if maybe there was time left for him to fulfill that dream. Despite the terminal diagnosis, Henry and Valetta felt as if the Lord was leading them to join an international mission agency. Henry was in remission long enough to take a trip around the world, but like the title of his book, *Mission Accomplished: Under Sentence of Death*, he knew that his days were numbered. While speaking in Korea he exclaimed, "I preach as a dying man to dying men."[16] Valetta remembers praying, "Lord, there are 500 missionaries here praying for his healing. Surely that's enough to heal my husband!"[17] but that night as Henry lay next to her in bed and Valetta prayed for his healing, she heard God's words in her heart, "I'm going to heal him, but not in the way that you are thinking. Soon Henry's healing will be total and eternal."[18] Five days after they returned from their trip around the world, Henry made his final trip to meet his Savior.

Valetta had to walk through the valley again. She went through a time of depression and loneliness. She cried out to God, recognizing that she was not experiencing the abundant life that Jesus promised.

"My life is not abundant right now," she gasped as she asked herself why. She describes how she felt:

> I began to realize that I didn't have faith to believe God could take care of everything in my life. . . . That's when I learned in the hard places of my life to draw closer to God. I began to really understand how to be filled with the Holy Spirit. Because the Holy Spirit can't fill you when you want to plan your own life, I began to ask God to forgive me for trying to run my own life, to take over, and fill me with His Spirit.[19]

Now, a single mom to two small kids, she assembled a life for the three of them, working at the headquarters of One Mission Society. One day her son, Leon, surprised her when he noticed, "Mother, you are smiling again!" Valetta explained, "That's because I've trusted Jesus with everything."[20] Several years later, Leon graduated from high school and went off to college. One weekend, he returned home to Greenwood, Indiana bringing a college buddy for a visit. Later that evening Leon, his friend, and his sister Lorna decided to go bowling with the youth group. Valetta fed them and then waved goodbye as they drove off. A while later, she received a knock on her door. When she pulled it open, she found a police officer standing in front of her. Gravely, he explained to her that because the temperature had dropped, the rain had turned to ice. A patch of black ice had caused a terrible car accident, and her children had not survived. The shock was immense. At first, she felt as if she was just dangling in space, but then suddenly she describes an overwhelming feeling as if the arms of Jesus were holding her.

This makes it three times through the valley. She shares that if she hadn't known Jesus was with her or if she hadn't had her anchor in God's Word, she could not have gone on. Her whole identity as a wife and now mother had been ripped away, leaving her wondering, "Who am I?" She struggled to consider where she should go from here. Was there anything else for her? She wondered whether to resume her call to missions alone. She described that decision this way, "As I prayed, I began thinking, 'What job could I do that would help the most people come to Christ?'"[21] She felt like the answer was to stay in missions. She focused on God's goodness and decided to go overseas and serve. Valetta experienced various tests of her faith while serving cross-culturally. One particularly difficult test happened in Taiwan when she was attacked and raped in her home. That rapist was arrested and convicted. He had raped and killed many women. Now on death row, Valetta, along with a Chinese coworker, took the opportunity to witness to him and share the invitation that Christ offers all of us of forgiveness and redemption. She praised the Lord for an opportunity to talk with him and thanked God for the gift of a forgiving heart. She recognized that only God is the one who could give her a heart of compassion for this young man who was destroyed by Satan.

She relates that throughout that time, "I began to realize that God uses even these kinds of things, and I believe that He triumphed over the evil and took the fear out of my heart."[22] She made the choice to trust in the goodness of God and let Him take control though all her losses. Through her story, Valetta inspires us to look at adversity from God's perspective. She encourages us to see suffering not as why did God allow this, but how will God use this redemptively in my life? Reflecting on her life she shares, "The road of suffering has been a journey for me. The question of suffering is a big one and God is the answer to it."[23]

How is it that some people are able to walk through unthinkable suffering and emerge proclaiming God's goodness? Valetta's story of surrender challenges me to view life with a different perspective. The only explanation for how she walked through the deep darkness is her assuredness in the character of God. Despite her situation, she was absolute in her conviction of the goodness of God. Her roots are roots of truth. The root that God is good brings a certainty into Valetta's thoughts that no calamity can change. Her life proclaims; God is good!

God's goodness is in His nature, and that goodness is not a reflection of how things are going in our lives. The choice to believe in His goodness is one we make in the midst of our grief and loss. Simultaneously, we acknowledge the pain we are feeling and in faith lean into His goodness. He is with us when we experience the pains of rejection, loss, sickness, and utter grief. No matter what happens in our lives, He never leaves us. We can see His goodness in the life of Jesus. After his friend Lazarus died, Jesus arrived late at the scene. Mary fell at his feet and, with gut-wrenching sobs, declared that if He had been there, her brother would not have died. Jesus was "*deeply moved in spirit* [*to the point of anger at the sorrow caused by death*] *and was troubled*" (John 11:33 AMP), and He wept. It was a visceral reaction. He was furious with death. Jesus hates evil and had a deeply internal emotional response. He fully grasped the pain his friends were carrying and entered right into it with them. His tears flowed. His heart ached alongside theirs.

Because we already know the story, we know that in just a few more verses He is going to raise Lazarus from the dead. So, we ask, why? Why would Jesus cry? There is no reason to cry. Soon, all those tears of sadness will be turned to tears of joy. He could have just told everyone to stop and explain there was no need to cry, but He didn't. He loved His friends and chose to sit in grief with them. This is who God is—He feels empathy with His people. In her book, *Simple*

Obsession, Jamie West Zumwalt explains, "This is God's character. Jesus understood all that Mary was feeling—the grief, the confusion, the anger. He felt all of it with her. He loved her, and he hated seeing her in so much pain. He wept with her."[24] God is good, and He cares for us. He is not distant. Even though He knows that our problems are temporary, He doesn't tell us to just get over it, deal with it, and move on. He is profoundly moved by what we are going through and weeps along with us. He is good.

Because we live in a fallen world, life will bring pain and difficulties. We will all be tempted to let our thoughts, feelings, and behavior shift our confession that God is good to the lie that God is not good. The lie grabs hold of us, and we are duped. Since we know the truth about God, we assume that we are believing it. We quote the Bible verse Romans 8:28, "*we know that in all things God works for the good of those who love him, who have been called according to his purpose*," but inside a hollowness sits in our stomach. Satan's strategy blinds us, and we do not see the lie. He tries to make it no big deal, prompting us to tell ourselves that we don't really believe God isn't good. But check out your thoughts because your habitual thoughts display what you are believing. Those thoughts are your poisonous berries, and they are being sustained by the lie underneath. We all need to acknowledge that this root lie, God is **not good** could be lurking underneath, feeding our thoughts.

My thoughts of what if regarding my child's health, our finances, work problems, relationship conflicts, my abilities, and so on have shown me that I am full of fear and not full of faith. The origins of my negative thoughts are so extremely contrary to God's character. They are the opposite! Sure, I say I believe that God is good, God is trustworthy, God loves me, and God is enough. However, it's not my words that reveal what I believe; it is how I live that reveals what I believe. As my grandmother would say, "The proof is in the pudding."

Listening for Truth

1. How have you answered the question: If God is good, why doesn't He do good in my life?
2. Ask yourself if there is any past disappointment that you might be hanging on to that is causing a barrier between you and God.
3. Consider God's goodness in your life. He has been with you in your pain. If you aren't able to see it, ask God to show you where and how.
4. Is it possible that you have the root lie that God is not good? Spend some time considering your berries and asking yourself what could be feeding them.

Chapter 14

THE ROOT LIE: GOD IS NOT TRUSTWORTHY

When our daughter was old enough to attend school, she was so excited. She actually cried on the weekends because she missed being at school. She loved it so much! That is why I was surprised when she came home one day and announced that she did not want to go back to school. She was adamant that she would not return. I couldn't understand what had happened until later, when her brother told me that there had been a fire drill that day. As we were getting ready for bed that night, we talked about it, and she shared how scared she had been because she thought it was real. I assured her that these were just for practice and that there wouldn't be a real emergency when the alarm sounded, but that she needed to practice with her classmates so they could be prepared. She seemed to understand, and her anxiety subsided. She was willing to go back to school. Unfortunately, a few days later, the school did a lockdown drill. That was it for her, and she decided she would not return. I asked her if she would like to go through the Berry Bush together. We labeled her fear of drills as her poisonous berry. As we worked through her thoughts, feelings, and behavior, and asked why throughout the conversation, we eventually got down to her root lie, which was a wrong belief about God. We talked about what it feels like in her body when she imagines the drill and then what her mind is thinking when she feels worried. Instead of drawing a Berry Bush, she drew a picture of how she feels when she thinks about the drill. She explained her drawing to me as we talked. Our conversation went something like this:

Daughter: (Pointing to her drawing) This is me holding my tummy because when I think about the drill, my tummy hurts, and I feel like my heart is pounding fast. My mind is thinking that the teachers won't keep me safe.

Me: What do you mean, won't keep you safe?

Daughter: I will get hurt, and they won't be able to help me.

Me: Why won't they help you?

Daughter: I am all alone. See, here I am all by myself (points to her drawing).

Me: Why do you feel like you are all alone?

Daughter: There is no one to keep me safe.

Me: Have you thought about God being there with you?

Daughter: God can't help me because I can't see Him.

Me: Yes, I understand what you mean when you say you can't see Him, but remember that God is always with you. He never leaves you. Even though you can't see Him with your eyes, He is always with you.

Daughter: If He is there, God won't help.

Me: Why do you say that?

Daughter: I don't believe that God is going to help me. I can't trust God.

We found her root lie: God is not trustworthy. Even though she knew stories about God's faithfulness, had sung songs of His trustworthiness, and memorized verses, she was still struggling to believe it. As we finished, we sang a song called "I can trust God" by Lifekids.[1] I reminded her to sing it whenever she starts to feel worried about a possible drill. As we cleaned up the crayons, I thought, "Fantastic! This Berry Bush really works even when you are little. However, later that evening, she came to me and said, "I am still worried. I don't want to trust God." Nothing I said or did could convince her. Wanting to help her, I felt frustrated. I knew that she could lighten up her worry by recognizing her fear as a lie; however, I could totally relate to her. I feel that same way sometimes myself. I know the truth, and I recognize that I am not living in the truth, but I don't want to stop listening to the lie. I don't feel like I can move out of it. I want to stay here and worry.

Fear of Finances

She is not the only one who struggles with the root lie that God is not trustworthy. Look how my Berry Bush grows when my poisonous berry is the anxiety of finances. Here is my conversation with myself:

Me: We have no money, and I am freaking out!

Inner Voice: Why am I afraid?

Me: I'm afraid of not having enough money for the future.

Inner Voice: Why?

Me: I won't be able to provide.

Inner Voice: Why are you afraid of not being able to provide?

Me: I don't know how I'll be able to survive.

Inner Voice: Why?

Me: Because we need money and it's up to me and my husband to provide it.

Inner Voice: Why do I feel like it's up to me?

Me: I don't believe God will provide.

Inner Voice: Why do I think that God won't provide?

Me: Because I can't trust Him.

Inner Voice: Why can't you trust Him?

Me: That's it! I found my root lie—God is not trustworthy.

Figure 2. Berry Bush: God Is Not Trustworthy

Reader, maybe you can relate to my fear of finances. I know that my Berry Bush is not the only bush with the fear of finances berry ripening on it. I recently saw on the news that 77 percent of Americans are anxious about finances.[2] There are a lot of us struggling. It's easy for us to acknowledge that God is sovereign, but can we trust Him with our finances? That question sounds silly, but this is something all of us must face. If we are going to say that God is trustworthy, then let's live out our conviction of His trustworthiness. When I was six years old, I began singing in my little country church. Back then, we would have "special music" before the preacher began his sermon. I would stand up on a chair behind the pulpit and belt out hymns. One favorite of mine was the song, "God Said It, I Believe It, That Settles It."[3] Toward the end of the chorus, the song poses a question similar to this; I'm choosing to believe what is true. What about you? It is a choice. When we are faced with a difficulty, we have to decide whether we will see it as a problem or as an opportunity to see God work. If we choose not to see it as an opportunity, we should stop and ask ourselves, what truth about who God is am I finding hard to believe in this moment?

What Part of God's Heart Am I not Fully Trusting?

I boarded my flight from Dallas to Orlando and found my assigned seat next to a beautiful Kenyan woman. I asked her what she had been doing in Dallas. She told me that her decision to come had been inspired by a question her husband had asked her, "What part of God's heart are you not fully trusting?" She explained that she had been wanting to come to take a class she needed to start a new job, but had thought it impossible because of finances. Even though she had found an unbelievably low airplane ticket online, she had written off the idea of the trip because she knew she could not afford housing. She was telling her husband about her disappointment at not being able to attend, and that is when he called her out with his question: What part of God's heart was she not fully trusting? He reminded her, "You trust God. You have trusted Him in the past, and I know that you want to trust Him now. He will provide, just wait and see." She went on to explain how her husband was right. A few days later, an envelope came in the mail with a check. She couldn't believe it was more money than she had hoped for, but she doubted that the check was genuine. When she went to the bank, she held her breath as she handed it to the cashier, figuring that it was all a hoax, but it wasn't. The money was deposited into her account, and she was astounded. She began to praise God right there in the lobby. Her husband explained to her that they had somehow overpaid a bill and that the money was a reimbursement to them. That is how God worked it all out for her to come to Dallas to attend the training and begin her new career. She shared with me, "I know that I can trust God, so why do I doubt Him?" We spent the rest of the flight considering that question.

Jennie Allen describes in her book, *Get Out of Your Head*, how she doubted God's trustworthiness. She battled for eighteen months with fearful thoughts that would wake her up at night, terrified, questioning everything about God and her life with Him. She walks us through her story, explaining how she finally shared what was happening with friends, how they helped her see it was a spiritual battle, and how she found freedom. She confessed that during that time she believed that she was a victim to her thoughts and urges us not to fall for that lie. Acknowledging how difficult it is to take every thought captive in every situation, Jennie explains:

> Learn to take *one* thought captive and, in doing so, affect every other thought to come. So what is the one thought that can successfully interrupt every negative thought pattern? It's this:
>
> I have a *choice.*
> That's it.
> The singular, interrupting thought is this one:
> I have a *choice.*[4]

Noah had a choice. God presented him with the craziest task ever conceived: to build a massive ark so that he, his family, and all the animals could come on board to survive a global flood. He had to build this colossal monstrosity in the middle of dry land. It took years to construct, and he had to do it in his community where surely his wicked neighbors mocked him! What kind of thoughts must he have had? The Bible doesn't tell us, but it does tell us that "*Noah did everything as the Lord commanded him*" (Genesis 7:5 NLT). He made his choice. He chose not to listen to lies. He chose to obey. His obedience to God was evidence of his faith. His life communicated his trust in God. In the plans he shared with Noah, He did not include instructions about building a rudder or steering mechanism. Noah's job was simply to build the ark and let the Lord take it from there. Most of the plan was unknown to him. That is what it looks like to follow God, to live in the unseen. We know that He is trustworthy, and that is all that we need to know. When we have a proper understanding of who God is, it will birth faith inside us. Although there was evil all around him, "*Noah found favor in the eyes of the Lord*" (Genesis 6:8). The Bible paints a picture of a deeply corrupt culture in Noah's day. Still, Noah refused to let his surroundings define him. He looked to who God is and chose to walk with Him. We're invited to do the same, no matter what's happening around us.

Sometimes, our circumstances cause us to question God's trustworthiness. Everything that is happening around us wants to dictate our attitude, but we have a choice. Dr. Chris Thurman reminds us, "God doesn't always intervene in our circumstances, but He always intervenes in our minds if we let Him."[5] I was listening to a podcast[6] recently and heard the testimony of a man who waited for God to move and heal his wife, but that is not what happened. God did not heal her. God did not change his reality, but He did intervene in his mind.

This is the story of Chris Hilke, professor of theology and apologetics at Summit Bible College and the Senior Pastor at College Ave Church in San Diego, California. Chris met Paige in college and was immediately smitten. Paige, on the other hand, wasn't interested, at least not at first. He tried everything from small gifts to flowers, but it was his offer of guitar lessons that finally won her over. In June of 2013, just ten days after she had won the national championship in softball and graduated summa cum laude, they married. A little over seven years later, they had five kids, and together they had built a beautiful family. However, it wouldn't be long before the unimaginable would happen. After the birth of their fifth child, Paige's back began to hurt, and the pain was eventually traced to a pulmonary embolism. When the doctor explained the diagnosis, terror filled her heart. Two mothers she followed on Instagram had recently died from the same condition, and the weight of that knowledge pressed in on her. Unable to shake the belief that she was dying, she couldn't sleep. After days without rest, her mind grew exhausted and vulnerable, and she began struggling with suicidal thoughts.

Eventually, she and Chris decided that it was in the best interest of the whole family for her to enter an inpatient treatment center. Around ten o'clock one morning, while the kids were contentedly playing, Chris's phone rang just like it had every day since Paige had entered the center. Chris excitedly picked it up, expecting to hear Paige's voice on the other end. Instead, it was her psychiatrist, a lawyer, and the president of the inpatient center calling to tell him that his wife had "made an attempt on her life and she was successful."[7] Chris processed their words, realizing that they were telling him that his wife had died. She was gone.

He was left alone to raise his five children, ages six, four, three, two, and four months old. Grief overwhelmed him. He had expected God to give his wife back to him. He felt like if God was going to take someone that He would take someone deserving of it, but not Paige, his wife and mother of his children. He was a pastor who dedicated his life to teaching God's word. Why? Chris confesses that he was so angry. He had expected God to keep them safe and fix everything by bringing his wife back home healthy. However, after having fasted, prayed, and pleaded with the Lord daily to free her, Chris explains, "The answer was unequivocally no. So now I've got two options: I can either rip up this idea of God that I had, and allow him to replace it with a real one, or I'm going to have to rip up God."[8]

As an apologist, Chris had already explored other worldviews and found them bankrupt. He knew that his only option was to lean into Jesus, recognizing that he had nothing. Everything had been shaken. He had lost his identity. He didn't have anything else to turn to. He shared how he approached God, "I'm going to need you to rebuild my paradigm of who you are. It can be raw and unfiltered and messed up because the copacetic sanitized version of you is dead, the one that doesn't let anything bad happen to people."[9] He felt like he had come to God with a simple request, to save his wife. He hadn't asked Him for something extravagant and unreasonable, yet God had not given him what he had asked. Chris explained, "I had to just reframe everything and meet Jesus again for the first time."[10] As he did, he let "Jesus explain who he was in a way that was realer and more colorful and beautiful than he ever was before."[11] Chris has had opportunities to share his story of heartache and of God's trustworthiness. As he shares his story, he has noticed how often people struggle with questions about whether God can be real, good, or loving in the face of terrible suffering. Thinking back through his own story, he points out, "It's so interesting that that's the first emotional response I had—there must not be a God, or if he is, he's not one worthy of my worship."[12] Chris recognized that thought in his head for the lie that it was, straight from the devil, and chose instead to do away with the façade of the unbiblical version of Jesus and seek out the true Jesus. God did not undo the devastation Chris faced, yet He stepped into Chris's mind, convincing him of His reality and trustworthiness. Chris continues to live from that truth. We can live out the truth of God's faithfulness too, when we recognize that we no longer have to surrender to the thoughts born from the lie that God is not trustworthy. We will choose to stop permitting those blasphemous lies to occupy space in our heads and instead meditate on true thoughts that remind us of our God, who is our provider, our protector, our healer, our helper, our all-sufficient God, and He is trustworthy.

Trusting in His Trustworthiness

That night in the upper room when Jesus shared His last supper with the disciples, He wanted to teach them a lesson about humility and self-sacrifice. He got up from the table and began going from disciple to disciple, washing their feet. When he came to Peter, he refused to allow Jesus to perform the task of a lowly servant: "*Jesus answered him, What I am doing you do not understand now, but afterward you will understand*" (John 13:7 ESV). So many things happen in our lives that we do not understand. We feel perplexed just as Peter did. We want to tell Jesus, "No way!" but He assures us that, although we don't understand right now, one day we will. When we get to Heaven, the perspective of eternity will make everything clear. We will see how God was working out His beautiful, loving plan through all the difficult and painful moments that we walked through here on earth. We can trust that He knows us completely; He knows things we don't know, sees things we don't see, and understands things that we don't fully understand. He is always working for our good and His glory. We can trust Him! Let's make sure our thoughts remind us of His trustworthiness. Watch out for any berries that might lead to the root lie that God is not trustworthy. We want to make it known that we trust Jesus not just to save us from our sins, but also to be with us in every area of our lives, in every decision, in every relationship, and in every hard circumstance. Everyone around us will see that our God is trustworthy by the way we live out our lives.

Something our family started doing every New Year's Day is celebrating "stones of remembrance" together, based on the Bible story in Joshua 4. This is where God commanded the Israelites to take twelve stones from the Jordan River bed after they had crossed it on dry ground. These stones were to serve as a memorial, reminding them and future generations of how God had miraculously parted the river, allowing them to cross on dry land. These stones offer an opportunity to tell of God's power and faithfulness. They speak of the trustworthiness of our God. I go to the local craft store and buy some smooth rocks and some fun permanent markers. Then on New Years Day, we gather at the table with a big bowl in the middle, full of years of memories of God's faithfulness. We can see all the ways that He has come through for us throughout the years. Each of those stones bears the record of how God has proven his trustworthiness to us. Whenever I need to remind myself, I pick up a few stones and hold them in my hand. I read the scrawled letters penned when our children were little, things like "car" when we didn't have money to buy one but our older minivan had bitten the dust, and we were desperate. Another rock is labeled "friends" when we had moved again and had to start over with building community in a new city. Some say "job," "school," "debt," or have names of people God put in our path. Each stone represents a significant memory of how God has answered our prayers. We leave this bowl of stones out on display to remind us all that God is trustworthy. We can trust Him!

Recently, we attended an end-of-year ceremony at our children's school. I knew that our daughter was up for some award, but I didn't know which one. I was amazed when the presenter began to read Jeremiah 17:7, "*Blessed is the one who trusts in the Lord, whose confidence is in Him.*" She described the award as honoring one student who exemplifies faithful confidence in words and actions. She then called out our daughter's name! The same one who had told me that she chose not to trust God, but wanted to worry. The teacher brought her up to the stage and continued to describe the Faithful Confidence Award, saying, "This recipient demonstrates a profound reliance on God as their foundation, showcasing a spirit of grace and compassion in their interactions, which inspires a supportive and loving environment within our school community." Wow! I had dropped the whole Berry Bush conversation with her. I hadn't wanted to push her or make her feel like she had to say what I wanted her to say. We enlisted help with a play therapist and, with new tools in her toolbelt and the repetition of many school drills, she is learning to face them. Several school years have come and gone since our original Berry Bush conversation. During that time, something beautiful has unfolded—our daughter's journey with Jesus is bringing her to a place where she now hangs her artwork on the fridge, reminding us by painting in bold, colorful letters that "God is with you!" She has made her choice. She chooses to believe that God is trustworthy. Now, how about you?

Listening for Truth

1. Have you ever felt like our little girl, knowing that you are believing a lie, but you don't want to stop listening to it?
2. Is fear of finances something growing on your Berry Bush? How does it play out in your thoughts, feelings, and behavior?
3. What part of God's character are you struggling to trust?
4. What kinds of stones of remembrance could help you when you are listening to the lie that God is not trustworthy?

Chapter 15

THE ROOT LIE: GOD DOESN'T LOVE ME

Perfectionism seems to be in my family's DNA. All our kids have struggled with it. My husband likes to say that he is a recovering perfectionist. Soon after we married, I was feeling down because of all the expectations I was putting on myself. It was obvious to me that I was an imperfect spouse. My husband tried to console me with the line, "It's just good to know that you are not perfect." He works to help all of us understand that we do not have to be perfect. He made some cards to pass out like business cards that he calls "Fail Cards," and he passes them out to our family and his team at work. He tells us that he wants to see us turn them in because he wants us to feel the freedom to fail. Perfectionism is not a mindset that is easy to shake off. Finding value in what we achieve and how we perform is so enticing to us. However, it leaves us empty and full of shame when we fail. Failure is a big berry for us. As I worked through my fear of failure, I realized that my root lie, the origin of all my anxiety, is that God doesn't love me. Here is an example of a conversation I had with my husband as we worked together to get down to my root lie:

> Me: I am worried about the meeting tomorrow.
>
> Paul: Why are you worried?
>
> Me: I am afraid that I will mess up and not say the right thing.
>
> Paul: Why?
>
> Me: I feel like everyone else is smarter and has it together. I am barely able to keep up.
>
> Paul: Why do you feel like that?
>
> Me: I feel like I'm going to fail.
>
> Paul: Why does that scare you?
>
> Me: Other than utter humiliation, I feel like God will be embarrassed
>
> Paul: Why?
>
> Me: I only feel worthy when I do a good job.
>
> Paul: Why do you think you feel like that?
>
> Me: I feel like God only loves me if I always do a good job.
>
> Paul: Why?
>
> Me: I feel like God doesn't love me unconditionally.

We found my root lie: God doesn't really love me.

Figure 3. Berry Bush: God Doesn't Love Me

Underneath my perfectionism is a deep fear that if I don't measure up and prove myself worthy, God won't truly love me. That ugly lie permeates my thinking and controls how I parent, treat my spouse, run meetings at work, interact with coworkers, act at church, and think about myself. This root lie that God does not love me affects everything.

Belly Button Focus

When we have the spotlight on ourselves, all we can do is worry. We feel anxious about what we don't have, what we want, what we need to be, and so on. Self has struck again. We have fallen once more for our biggest problem, making self the lord of our life. We are held captive by it. Self dominates our every thought, feeling, and action, bringing doubt, confusion, and panic. After many years of digging down through these roots, I have realized that my feeder roots are all about me. Me, me, me. The fears that plague me and take over my thinking are all fears driven by self. Our family has labeled this propensity to put self first as being "belly-button focused." When you are staring at your navel, all you can think about is yourself, your needs, your wants, and your perspective. With your center of vision fixated on self, everyone and everything else is blurred. Being "belly-button focused" keeps you from seeing all that God wants to show you. He created you in your mother's womb and gave you that belly button to remind you that you are connected to others. And you are connected to Him. This symbol of our beginnings marks our bodies, reminding us that we are His. He is our creator and loves us. Self can lead us to think otherwise. We compare ourselves to others. We look around and think God must really love them, but not me. I don't have what they have. We confuse material possessions and successful human relationships as proof of God's love for us. Self either tells us that we deserve more or that we don't deserve anything. Both perspectives, a high self-esteem or a low self-esteem, come from a belly button focus.

Dr. Chris Thurman makes it clear, "There is no such thing as self-worth. There is only God-worth. And given that God fearfully and wonderfully makes everyone in His image, everyone has the same permanent, never-going-to-be-higher-or-lower worth."[1] God loves us and calls us worthy. We will only find our worthiness in Him. Yet, self convinces us to rely on pride to navigate our way through this life. We depend on pride to survive when we have thoughts that lead to feelings such as "nobody loves me," "I'm all alone," "I don't have what it takes," "I'm stupid," "I'll never get things right," and "I'm worthless." Pride is handling it all for us, whether it is belittling us with how undeserving, shameful, and contemptible we are, or it is showing off and bragging to others about how "with it" we are. Self attempts to fill the space that belongs to God. The self way leads to death. The only way to live is the Jesus way. However, following Him is costly, "*Whoever wants to be my disciple must deny themselves and take up their cross and follow me*" (Matthew 16:24). Self life is protecting self at all costs, but following Jesus means daily choosing to put self to death. "Nobody who follows Jesus can hold on to even the smallest bit of their own agenda, their own dreams, their own way of living in the world. They must sacrifice every ounce of self if they would choose to walk after Him."[2] Taking up our cross is a moment-by-moment decision to live not for self, but for Christ. The devil tells us that denying ourselves equals being miserable, that it means depriving myself of the things that make me who I am, my dreams, personality, and what I love. However, Jesus promises that when I deny myself, I will not lose myself; instead, I will find myself.

Peter's Example of Self Taking Over

Not wanting us to be secure in God's love, Satan reminds us of the importance of saving self. This is what happened to Peter. Known for his boldness, he started out strong, declaring Jesus as the "*Christ, the Son of the living God*" (Matthew 16:16 ESV). However, just a few verses later, after Jesus states that He is about to suffer and go to the cross willingly, we see Peter listening to self, challenging Jesus, and trying to impose his own desires:

> *Peter took him aside and began to reprimand him for saying such things. "Heaven forbid, Lord," he said. "This will never happen to you!" Jesus turned to Peter and said, "Get away from me, Satan! You are a dangerous trap to me. You are seeing things merely from a human point of view, not from God's."*
>
> —Matthew16:22–23 NLT

As Peter processed Jesus's words that He would soon suffer and be killed, Peter's thoughts propelled him to listen to his own disappointment in Jesus. He began to realize that Jesus would not fulfill his idea of what the Messiah should be. Frustration overcame him, and Peter was stuck in thoughts of self. Jesus rebukes Peter, recognizing that Satan had influenced his thinking. Peter's thoughts had opened him up to becoming the mouthpiece of the enemy, a participant in the Adversary's plan to divert Jesus from the cross. When Peter's expectations were not met, his confusion caused him to think like the world thinks. However, Jesus got his attention and informed him, "*These thoughts of yours don't come from God, but from human nature*" (Matthew 16:23 GNT). "You're not thinking as God thinks. You're strictly seeing things from a human perspective, and you are a stumbling block. You are trying to hinder Me from fulfilling God's plan." Peter's vision for what the Messiah would and would not be took over his thoughts, and self got in the way. His problem with self taking control occurred again the night that Jesus was arrested. Jesus had warned Peter:

> *"Simon, Simon, look out! Satan has asked to sift you like wheat. But I have prayed for you that your faith may not fail. And you, when you have turned back, strengthen your brothers."*
>
> *"Lord," he told Him, "I'm ready to go with You both to prison and to death!" "I tell you, Peter," He said, "the rooster will not crow today until you deny three times that you know Me!"*
>
> —Luke 22:31–34 HCSB

Peter thought he was strong. He promised Jesus, "*Even if everyone else deserts you, I will never desert you*" (Matthew 26:33 NLT). Peter's pride kept him from realizing the spiritual reality that Jesus wanted him to understand. Temptation was coming, the biggest he had faced, and he was about to fail. He would fail not just once, but three times! After Judas and the armed crowd with him took Jesus away, Peter followed at a distance, watching. He stood warming himself at a charcoal fire, and it was there that he was recognized as one of Jesus's disciples. Three different times, people came to him, affirming that Peter had been with Jesus, even pointing out that his accent gave him away. Peter did just what Jesus said he would do; he disowned Him, swearing "*a curse on me if I'm lying—I don't know the man*" (Matthew 26:74 NLT)! When the rooster crowed, Jesus turned and looked at Peter. Overwhelmed with guilt and shame, Peter ran out weeping bitterly. The temptation to protect self had overcome him, taking over his emotions and controlling his behavior. Fear and panic resulted in betrayal and shame. After this happened, he would not be the same. If we were to "Berry Bush" Peter's fear, we could guess that his roots would sound like this: "Jesus could never forgive me for denying Him. I am not worthy to be considered His disciple anymore. I messed up too badly. The voice in my head keeps reminding me that I am too far gone. It's too late. I'll never be good enough." That berry could have grown and flourished. The shame could have held him captive.

However, Jesus would not let that happen. After His resurrection, He made sure to remove that shame. The Gospel of John tells us how; after his disciples decided to go fishing and caught nothing all night, Jesus appeared to them. He wanted to restore what was broken between Him and Peter. He stood on the shore and called out to them, advising them to cast their net on the other side of the boat. When John told Peter, "*It's the Lord!*" (John 21:7), Peter jumped into the water to swim to Jesus. As soon as he saw so many fish in the net, he remembered that this was exactly what Jesus had done when He first called him to be His follower (Luke 7). Jesus was recreating that scene for him. He was sending Peter a message: "No matter how badly you think you failed, I want you to know that this relationship is still open. You are not too far gone." Jesus is not condemning him, recounting all the ways that Peter failed Him. Nor is He treating him harshly. No, Jesus is reminding him of their relationship and how much He loves him.

Maybe you have felt like Peter. I know that I have. I have felt that the selfish, blatantly sinful choices I made had caused me to be too far from God. My actions and attitude had been so wrong that there was no way to get back to God. I thought there was no reason to pray because He wouldn't want to hear from such a weak, floundering failure anyway. I tried to hide and steer clear of God, thinking that "He would never want to be around me." I surrounded myself with a wall of shame. However, Peter didn't react like me. He rushed toward Jesus, throwing himself into the water. Once on shore, he found Jesus cooking breakfast on a charcoal fire. A charcoal fire that would forever be ingrained in his mind. He had stood over a charcoal fire to warm himself that night, the night he betrayed Jesus. Peter's thoughts had to be trying to pull him down, but Jesus was showing him, "I still love you!" He cooked them breakfast with some of their freshly caught fish, and together they ate.

Afterward, addressing the shame Peter felt for denying Him three times, He asked him a question, the same question three times: "*Do you love me?*" (John 21:15–17). By doing this, He prompted Peter to do some self-reflection. He gave Peter three opportunities to confess his love for Him. Now, Peter was different; he had changed. This is not the same brash, arrogant Peter comparing his love for Christ with everyone else's. Now, he knew the truth about himself, and Peter responded humbly: "*Lord, you know I love you*" (John 21:15–17). The repetition of Jesus's question "*Do you love me?*" grieved Peter, but with this question, Jesus reversed Peter's three denials into three clear confessions of love. Jesus wouldn't let him stay in that state of self-condemnation but lovingly reassured him that he was forgiven and that He deeply desired to be in a relationship with him. There was no reason for shame. He pointed out to Peter that he had a job. Instead of being a fisherman, He reminded Peter that he was a fisher of men (Matthew 4:19). Through this conversation, he showed Peter that He trusted him and commissioned him to lead and serve His sheep, to feed them and care for them. Jesus then restated the precise phrase He had used when He first asked Peter to be His disciple, "*Follow me*" (Matthew 4:19).

The tender way that Jesus invited Peter to reflect on his love and commitment to Him demonstrates God's kindness and deep love for us. No matter how badly we fail Him, He still forgives us. We can count on His love. He will not give up on us: "*If we are faithless, He will remain faithful*" (2 Timothy 2:13). Because Jesus took our sin to the cross and defeated death, He made a relationship with God possible; now God sees us as clean and forgiven. He desires to be in a relationship with us. God is love; that is who He is. Even if you have a story like Peter's, that doesn't stop God. He is asking you, "Do you love me?" God's love is not dependent on what we do or don't do. God loves you, no matter what your mind tries to convince you about your past or mistakes. His love is not based on our actions at all. There is nothing we could do or not do to make Him love us. Love is who He is.

My Son Ben

God is love, but we can't feel His love when we are focused on self. Self gets in the way and tells us to keep trying to be or do something to earn love. That is how I got caught up in perfectionism and passed it on to my son Ben. I told you about him earlier. Anxiety has been his companion for much of his life. Ben is a PERFECTIONIST, and I type it in all caps on purpose. His struggle is deserving of using all capital letters to explain it. He battles with the idea of having to do everything right. He fights against anxiety because, of course, it is humanly impossible to do everything right all the time. His race in this life has been grueling as he continues to put one foot in front of the other while fears and "what-ifs" grab at his heels, attempting to trip him up. However, as I stand on the sidelines cheering him on, it has also been beautiful to see how God has been working in him throughout his journey. Ben is off at college now, and just recently he left me a voicemail sharing about what God has been teaching him as he continues to hack through the jungle of perfectionism and the anxiety it produces. In his message, he shared how he has made the connection of noticing when his anxiety appears. His deep, confident voice declared:

> My anxiety comes from a spotlight that I have on myself with all the pressure and perfectionism that I put on myself to be perfect. I say to myself, "Once I get this certain thing, I'll be OK. Once I get success in this area, I'll be fine." That's just a lie, a recipe for discontentment in my life. I don't want to be discontented or complacent, but I do want to have joy in the journey that I'm on and joy wherever I am.

Self wants Ben and all of us to keep the focus on ourselves, with everything and everyone else, including God, revolving around us. We know in our heads that God, not us, should be at the center of everything, but that is not how we live out our lives. Self causes me to view every circumstance and situation from my own perspective. I see the sun rising in the east and setting in the west, and think surely the sun revolves around me, but I need a different vantage point. The early astronomer Nicolaus Copernicus revolutionized science when he theorized that the accepted geocentric model of thinking was wrong. He proposed that the sun did not revolve around the Earth. Just as he removed the Earth from the center and placed the sun in the middle of the universe, we too need to remove self from the center of our universe. We need a "Spiritual Copernican Revolution."[3] Stop allowing self to limit your vision, convincing you that the spotlight is all on you, creating anxiety and pressure to perform.

Change your perspective to see that God is at the center, and recognize that your path revolves around Him. That is what He created you to do. Life is not about you; it is about Him. When Jesus came to earth, lived a sinless life, and died in our place, He took away all our pressure to be perfect. We should be living in freedom because we orbit Him.

In his message, Ben highlighted Jesus's words in the Sermon on the Mount about worry and anxiety: "*Is life not more than food, and the body more than clothes*" (Matthew 6:25)? He noted that immediately after telling the crowd not to worry, Jesus promised that when we "*seek first his kingdom and his righteousness*" (Matthew 6:33), God will provide what we need. I replayed the message to hear it again and listened as Ben acknowledged:

> The heavenly Father knows my needs. He knows what I need, and He loves me. I want to have a heart of love. I want God's love to be the center of my actions. In everything I do, I want to be living out of God's love. I want God's love to be the center of my universe, not myself, not my own desires, my wants or my needs. God's love. He knows my needs and my wants.

Yes! Ben is right. When we seek God first, allowing our mind to be transformed and our heart to be filled with His Kingdom priorities, we stop living for self. "To seek first the Kingdom of God means prioritizing love over survival."[4] Compelled to live a life of love, we are free from the fear of protecting self. Living this way reflects trust in God's character. We know that He loves us. We are convinced that He will take care of us because He values us greatly. We understand that He will provide all that we truly need to accomplish His will. Jesus brought God's kingdom on earth. In spite of all the injustice that happened in His life, the betrayal He suffered, the poverty He endured, and the violence He experienced, He remained secure in God's love and provision. When we seek first the kingdom of God:

> We'll stop competing with coworkers. We'll stop fretting about others' approval. We'll stop exhausting ourselves to secure a future we cannot control. The more we practice the ways of Jesus and his Kingdom, the more we enter a kind of freedom that helps us see how we are no longer in danger right now. God's got us. We are safe, and we are loved.[5]

When we seek first His kingdom and His righteousness, we shift the spotlight from illuminating our fear of self-preservation to shining the spotlight on the care and love of God—off self and onto God. When we move the light over to God, just as Ben expressed, God's love becomes the center of our universe. When we have ourselves in the center, our poisonous berries will keep growing and flourishing because our root lie is feeding them. It is not just the berry of perfectionism and fear of failure that is fueled by this root lie; there are more berries: past experiences, grief, hardships, mistakes, wounds inflicted by other Christians, feelings of insignificance, and so on. Our root lie is bolstering those berries with the lie that God doesn't love me. Deep in our belief system, this lie is impacting our thoughts, feelings, and behavior. This lie is hurting us, but we keep listening to it. If God really loved me . . .

Listening for Truth

1. Think of a time you found yourself being belly button focused. How did it affect your thoughts, feelings, and behavior?
2. Consider how Jesus treated Peter. How does He treat you?
3. Jesus is asking, "Do you love Me?" How do you answer?
4. Is it possible that you have the root lie that God doesn't love me? Spend some time considering your berries and asking yourself what is feeding them.

Chapter 16

THE ROOT LIE: GOD DOESN'T APPROVE OF ME

I hate it when my husband Paul says, "If I were you . . ." For some reason it just drives me bonkers. However, when he uttered those words, "If I were you Dawn, I would include a chapter with the root lie that God loves me but doesn't approve of me," I listened because this is Paul's root lie. He has lived with this lie, feeding his poisonous berries for years. He worked through the Berry Bush and dug way down to arrive at this root lie and has finally found freedom. That doesn't mean that these berries don't try to start growing again, but it means that when Paul realizes that a poisonous berry is in his mind, he is able to trace it down to the root and see it for the lie that it is. He doesn't mess around wasting time with the lie because he knows the truth.

Paul loves to help other people. He feeds on it. He looks for ways to help meet people's needs. He makes you feel like you are the most important person in the world when you talk with him. That is one of the reasons why I fell in love with him. He has a beautiful personality. However, there is a dark side to all this helping and people pleasing. When he is not in a healthy place, he gives of himself tirelessly, becoming deeply entangled in the lives of others, longing for their approval to reassure him of his worth. Deep down, he carries the quiet belief that, to be seen as enough in their eyes, he must somehow prove himself worthy. The root lie that God loves me but doesn't approve of me feeds his berries. Paul confesses, "Of course God loves me. That is His nature. That is who He is. I understand that, but I just can't bring myself to believe that God approves of me. This is a choice that I don't believe He makes. He wants me to know better, be better, do better, and He will not approve of me until I am more acceptable."

Here is an example of a conversation I had with Paul about something at work that was bugging him. This is how we worked together to get down to his root lie:

Paul: I am worried that my team will not be able to fill the personnel needs that we have.

Me: What makes that worry feel so strong?

Paul: I am afraid that I will disappoint leadership.

Me: Why does that scare you?

Paul: I need their approval.

Me: Why is their approval so important to you?

Paul: I need to be successful at work. I guess I find my worth in other's approval of my performance.

Me: Why is your value tied to your performance?

Paul: I feel like I need to do more and work harder to try to earn approval.

Me: Why are you trying to earn approval?

Paul: Because I am looking to my achievements to fulfill me and make people approve of me.

Me: Why are you looking for affirmation from people or accomplishments?

Paul: Because deep down, I don't feel like I have God's approval. Honestly, I feel like He just barely tolerates me.

Me: Why do you think that you feel that way about God?

Paul: My mind is telling me that God loves me, but He has to love me because He is God. I doubt that He likes me.

Me: Why do you think it's hard to believe that He truly likes you?

Paul: I'm constantly searching for approval from others, some kind of validation that I am worthy.

Me: Why do you think that's such a deep need for you?

Paul: Because while I feel like God loves me, I don't feel like He really approves of me.

We found Paul's root lie: God loves me, but He doesn't approve of me.

Figure 4. Berry Bush: God Doesn't Approve of Me

With this root lie we proclaim a half-truth, half of the totality of the gospel. Yes, God loves me. We know He loves us with perfect, unchanging, steadfast love through Jesus Christ, His Son. We know that nothing separates us from His love. Yet, that fear that God just barely tolerates us remains. It's like that thing we have heard a parent say to their kid, "I love you, but I don't like you right now." Is God saying that to us? Does God like me? Does He approve of me? When I question whether God likes me, could it be that I am trying to quantify how much He likes me? Is it possible for me to make God like me less through disobedience? Am I able to make God like me more through obedience? I know that is not scriptural, and that is not what is behind the question. The real question I am asking is, am I likable? Does God approve of me?

These questions are coming from a root lie that is a distorted view of God. The noxious root lie is that God has an overarching love for me but can't possibly approve of me. This lie tells me that God has looked me over and decided that He will not approve of me. I need to work harder, longer, better, be more dedicated and disciplined. Recently, Paul used AI to generate an image of what he hears as his inner voice. In the picture, we see Paul in a boat rowing furiously. At the stern is the coxswain, the person who calls out commands to the rowers. His face is full of rage as he shows his dissatisfaction with Paul's effort. The words hang above the image, "Work harder!"

Figure 5. Berry Bush: God Doesn't Delight in Me

Your Image of God

What is your image of God? How do you picture Him? All of us have images that carry emotional meaning for us. That is why, although you agree doctrinally that God accepts you and loves you, that He is good and loving, you might have a private image of God that is distorted. These images can influence our behavior without us even being conscious of it. These images impact our spiritual life because they barricade us off from God and others. They also correlate to how we see ourselves. For example, if we see God as impossible to please, we are likely to consider ourselves failures and tell ourselves we are just not good enough. Many of us deal with similar inner struggles about God. In a workshop called "Recovery from Distorted Images of God," Juanita R. Ryan shares, "I have observed in myself and in others that this kind of internal conflict about God is fairly common. It seems that people who believe in a God of love and compassion sometimes experience private images of God which are disturbing." [1] She explains that these images are uniquely personal. Still, they do tend to fall into certain categories such as too busy, abusive, unreliable, one who abandons, and the category that Paul's distorted image falls under—a god who does not accept you.

In his book *Healing for Damaged Emotions*, David Seamands describes an image of a god with impossible, demanding expectations. He sits up at the top of a tall ladder while you, wanting to please him, climb higher and higher, only to find that once you get there, he has moved up several rungs. So, you resolve to try harder, but when you reach those, he has already moved up another three rungs. For the person with this distorted image of God, they constantly have that inner voice replaying, "That's not quite good enough." [2] Seeking God's approval is never-ending because those poisonous berries have us confused, and the root lie is based on a distorted image of God—He disapproves of you. He doesn't like you. He finds you annoying.

My husband and I were recently on a long road trip, which gave us some rare, uninterrupted time to talk. As we drove down the highway, we shared about our Berry Bushes and our struggle with root lies. Paul began reflecting on the ongoing mental battle he has fought for years, caused by a berry he has labeled "Anxiety over difficult relationships." He has been excavating, pulling up more feeder roots, but he needed help to get to the root. As we drove down the highway, we dug together to reach the lie beneath. Our conversation went like this:

Paul: I struggle when I'm not in a good place with people, when I get sideways with them.

Me: Why does that affect you so much?

Paul: I don't like being wonky with people, feeling off or disconnected with them.

Me: Why do you think that unsettles you?

Paul: Because I really want people to like me.

Me: Why is it important that they like you?

Paul: I guess . . . I want them to truly enjoy me, for who I really am.

Me: Why do you feel such a need for them to enjoy you?

Paul: Because I want their validation.

Me: When you say "validation," what does that look like?

Paul: I want them to show they truly enjoy me, that they enjoy being with me. I crave that.

Me: Why do you crave it so much?

Paul: Honestly, I don't feel like I'm worthy of delight.

Me: Why do you feel unworthy of delight?

Paul: Deep down, I don't believe that God delights in me.

We found Paul's ugly root lie: God doesn't delight in me.

Does God Like Me?

I was listening to the podcast *Ask Pastor John*, when I heard this question come up, "I know God loves me, but does He like me?"[3] I'm sure John Piper's answer relieved the author of the question when he assured him that he is not the only one who had written in asking it. This is a common question. Many of us struggle with this root lie. We feel like we can never truly be liked, only tolerated. Our impression is that God only loves us because He must; He is God. Throughout our lives, others point out our shortcomings, and we begin to focus on them. We base our opinion of ourselves on our mistakes. Sometimes, we only see what we do wrong. In those moments we cannot imagine how God would look at us and be pleased. Piper suggests that for us to discover what it means to be enjoyed by God and be pleasing to Him, we need three things: an appreciation for the dimensions of God's love, a "Bible bath," and the work of the Holy Spirit.[4]

To understand what it means to be enjoyed by God, we first need to comprehend God's love for us, both His kindness that leads us to repentance and His delight in us. Piper explains:

> When God, by his love of benevolence, saves us and counts us righteous in Christ, and gives us the Holy Spirit, He

> begins a work of transformation that restores aspects of our personhood which are delightful to him, pleasing to him, which he genuinely likes about us. This is what God is doing in sanctification. You might say sanctification is God making us likable, pleasing.[5]

It is His work in us, renewing His image in us bit by bit. He is regenerating every part of us, our thoughts and desires, but it is a process. "God sees the incremental advances of our transformation by his Spirit and delights in them."[6] He looks on us with favor because of Christ's work in us. He is changing us, and we are becoming more like Him.

Sin

We have victory over sin in some places in our lives, but in other areas, we are still being refined. The Puritan theologian John Owens used the analogy of an impenetrable forest to describe sanctification.[7] This forest is dense, with the ground completely covered with twining vines, full of a tangled mass of undergrowth and overgrown brush. No light penetrates through to the soil. His analogy shows how sin dominates the entire landscape. However, when the Holy Spirit comes into our lives, He begins to create clearings and cleans out the thick brush. He takes a shovel to the poisonous Berry Bushes in our forest and excavates them, creating a clearing and uprooting them bit by bit. As He does so, He delights in us. We are delightful to God! "*The Lord delights in those who fear him, who put their hope in his unfailing love*" (Psalm 147:11). We please the Lord when we live in awe and reverence of Him; however, we don't begin life like that. Every one of us comes into this world fighting against God. No one is born wanting to do things God's way. We want to choose our own direction and live our lives on our own terms.

Besides enjoying how cute and adorable they are, having a toddler in the family provides a living example of how we, as humans, instinctively lean toward sinful choices. Because the ages of our kids are spread out, it seemed that a typical day gave me the opportunity to teach this truth often. When I heard a ruckus in the playroom, I knew it was only a matter of time before one of the older siblings would come to me and report that their younger brother or sister wasn't sharing, was being hurtful, or was otherwise misbehaving. "Of course they are!" I would respond. "You must teach them how to behave. You must model it for them so they can see it." They will not instinctively follow God because it is not natural. As humans, choosing sin is something we already know how to do. We came into the world that way. Our bent is selfishness.

Bible Bath

We don't have to be taught how to sin, but do have to be taught how to follow God. That is why Piper recommends bathing ourselves in Scripture.[8] As we seek to understand what it means to be pleasing to God, we will realize that a mind driven by self-interest and worldly pursuits cannot please God. *"And so people become enemies of God when they are controlled by their human nature; for they do not obey God's law, and in fact they cannot obey it. Those who obey their human nature cannot please God."* (Romans 8:7–8 GNT). We were in direct opposition to God and, without His grace, incapable of choosing God. Piper defines this as:

> Our hopeless condition. We were in an absolutely hopeless state apart from salvation. We never pleased God. He never liked what we did, because everything we did was not from faith. It was rooted in pride and rooted in selfishness and rooted in vainglory and seeking our own and ignoring him. That didn't please him at all.[9]

But God made a way for us to please Him. When Jesus took our sins upon Himself to die on the cross, He made it possible. When we choose to make Jesus our Lord, He will take away our fighting rebellious heart, give us a new heart, and send the Holy Spirit to empower us. Romans 8:9 tells us, "*You are not controlled by your sinful nature. You are controlled by the Spirit if you have the Spirit of God living in you*" (NLT). The Holy Spirit is transforming us, guiding us, and equipping us to live like Christ. His indwelling presence revolutionizes every aspect of our lives and is proof of God's love for us, "*For we know how dearly God loves us, because he has given us the Holy Spirit to fill our hearts with his love*" (Romans 5:5 NLT). The question, "Does God like me?" is answered by spending time soaking in the suds of a "Bible bath" where the Holy Spirit will awaken in you the truth about the magnitude of God's love, how He approves of you, is pleased with you, and how much He genuinely delights in who you are. Through the Holy Spirit, God invites you to experience His joy over you. He truly enjoys you. This is the truth that silences the awful lie growing on your Berry Bush and frees you from striving to earn His approval.

Beloved

The lie God disapproves of me is replaced with the truth that He delights in me, the truth that I bring joy to God's heart. He delights in the person He created me to be and truly enjoys who I am. He doesn't just tolerate me, He treasures me. God not only accepts me, He loves being with me. I fill God's heart with delight simply because I am His beloved child. Sarah Kroger sings a ballad called "Belovedness" [10] that I have playing on repeat as I write this section. It is a beautiful song that invites us to let go of our negative narratives, fear, and shame. It reminds us of how much our creator God loves us and that He made us just as we are and finds us beautiful. It calls us to replace our lies with His truth and let that define us because we truly are His beloved.

Before we were formed in our mother's womb, we were dearly loved. Our Creator marked us from our very beginnings as His beloved. It is who we are, our identity. Nothing else can define us, not our past failures, inadequacies, or tendency to compare ourselves. No one else gets to tell us who we are. God tells us that we are His. The truth that we are cherished will free us to let go of self-doubt, shame, and self-loathing and allow us to begin to see ourselves as His beloved. When we embrace this truth with our thought life, we will begin to live it out. "Becoming the Beloved means letting the truth of our belovedness become enfleshed in everything we think, say or do,"[11] explains Henri Nouwen in his book, *Life of the Beloved*:

> When our deepest truth is that we are the Beloved and when our greatest joy and peace come from fully claiming that truth, it follows that this has to become visible and tangible in ways that we eat and drink, talk and love, play and work.[12]

Our core has been marked as the beloved of God, and that truth is played out in every part of us: our thoughts, words, and actions. We are His, His beloved!

His Face Shines On Us

"Look at me, Mom! Look at me!" I hear my little daughter yelling out to me from across the pool. On our road trip, we stopped at a hotel, and soon after checking in and dumping our luggage in the room, we headed straight to the swimming pool. She absolutely loves swimming, and it means so much to her that I'm there to watch every moment. She'll dive beneath the water to show off her underwater flips and spins, hold perfectly still in her wobbly handstands, and then climb out, grinning, just to leap back in with a dramatic cannonball—sending water flying everywhere in her quest to make the biggest splash possible. All the while she is calling out, "Look at me! Mom, look at me!" I respond back, "I am looking. I see you! Wowee! You're doing great!" If I look away for even a moment, she notices immediately. She'll point two fingers at her own eyes, then back at me—a playful but firm reminder to keep my eyes on her. This audacious behavior comes to her naturally. There are many stories of how I, as a little girl, would take my father's face in my hands and turn it toward me when I wanted his attention (even when he was driving—yes, I was standing up in the front seat next to the driver—the '70s were a different time.) He always looked at me with a wide, gentle smile and eyes full of love. I never would have reached up to hold his cheeks and turn his attention toward my little face if there had been even a hint of sternness in his expression. We all want the face of our loved one to shine back at us with joy and to share that joy with them. We all want that connection. "God designed our brains for joy."[13] Joy with each other and joy with Him. Every Sunday at the end of our church worship service, the pastor leads us in the special blessing from Numbers 6:24–27: "*The Lord bless you and keep you; the Lord make his face shine on you and be gracious to you; the Lord turn his face toward you and give you peace.*" This is the same blessing that God gave to Moses for the priests to pray over God's people. This blessing is about God's face shining on us and lighting up with joy.

All of us are looking to be seen, known, and smiled on by God. In their book, *The Other Half of Church: Christian Community, Brain Science, and Overcoming Spiritual Stagnation*, Jim Wilder and Michel Hendricks expound on how God made us for joy. "He wants us to live in the glow of His delight. This blessing expresses a joy that can be paraphrased, 'May you feel the joy of God's face shining on you because He is happy to be with you.'"[14] God knows everything about us, yet He does not look at us with disgust and disappointment. He looks on us with delight and is glad to be with us. We don't have to call out or grab His cheeks. His face is always turned toward us. Consider Psalm 139:14–16:

> *I praise you because I am fearfully and wonderfully made; your works are wonderful, I know that full well. My frame was not hidden from you when I was made in the secret place, when I was woven together in the depths of the earth. Your eyes saw my unformed body; all the days ordained for me were written in your book before one of them came to be.*

He created this body, every part of it, inside and out. My brain, my neurodivergence, my face, my legs, my hair, my stomach, all these parts of me were made by His design. God doesn't think of me as ugly, strange, or weird. He made me. He gave me all these parts just the way He wanted, and He calls His work "very good." He also made me part of His body. Each of us is a different member, with distinct roles and giftings. He created me just like He wants me for a specific purpose. He doesn't just love me, He likes me.

We Are Puchinello

God approves of me, and I am special to Him. A book that embodies this idea is a children's book written by Max Lucado called *You are Special.* It tells the story of a small wooden boy named Punchinello. He lived among wooden people who constantly labeled one another with gold stars for success and gray dots for flaws. Covered in gray dots, Puchinello believed he was worthless. One day he met a stickerless wooden person who explained that the labels didn't stick to her because she spent time with their maker, Eli. When Punchinello visited Eli, he learned that others' opinions don't matter—only his maker's love matters. As he began to trust Eli's words, the stickers lost their power, and Puchinello's gray dots began to fall off.[15]

This is not just a story for children. It addresses everyone's need to understand that our Maker considers us special and approves of us. We work so hard to seek acceptance from God and others in vain. We don't need to try harder; God already approves of us. He is our maker. I love to read this story to my kids because it ministers to my heart with each reading. The reminder that no amount of gold stars or gray dots should matter to us hits me every time. As a people pleaser, I need that prompt to go back to the workshop and listen to my Maker, just like Punchinello did, so that my stickers will fall off. The more I trust that He accepts me, the less I will care about those stickers. I do not have to work to gain God's approval. I could never earn, achieve, or win His approval; He has already approved of me because of my relationship with Christ. He accepts me as His child despite all my flaws through Christ's sacrifice on the cross. Because of His grace, He fully and unconditionally accepts me. He has chosen to accept me in Christ to be holy and without fault in His eyes.

God Approves of Me

This fundamental truth—that God chooses to approve of me—is something that my husband Paul is living out today. That doesn't mean that his poisonous berries have stopped completely. They continue to show up occasionally. This happened just recently when some "misinformation" began circulating around the office about Paul and his team. Several departments began to feel slighted and didn't understand the current circumstances, so they began to blame Paul. Various rumors circulated about his lack of ability, and many started pointing fingers at Paul as the one to blame for their problems. As you can imagine, this situation had the potential for a real mental crisis for him. In the past, his identity had been so affected by his achievements at work. Now, with his approval rating lowering in the workplace, how would he react? His poisonous berry grew bigger, and he noticed his worried thoughts. Paul didn't want to give it any more of his attention, because he knew the source of those worries and fears. He recognized the ugly root lie, the lie about God that was feeding this poisonous berry. Because he had done the work to find his root lie, he had dug it up and replaced it with the truth. After he had excavated his root lie, he created a Truth Tree with the root truth: God approves of me. Connected to that root truth, Paul drew supporting roots that reminded him of God's approval of him. (In chapter 21, you will see Paul's drawing of his Truth Tree and get a chance to sketch out your own.)

Now, when others do not approve of him, it does not affect the truth that Paul chooses to focus on. He is able to move his thoughts to these supporting verses and others that pointed him to the truth that God approves of him. Living in the awareness that he is approved of by God, he doesn't have to toil or strive to seek approval. No. He is understanding his adoption in Christ, the fact that God chose him in Christ before the foundations of the earth. The gospel gives Paul the unwavering assurance that he is fully loved and divinely chosen by God. Now, the fruit on his Truth Tree, grown out of his root of truth—God approves of me—will mature and ripen into fruit that exhibits the following feelings: confident, accepted, validated, positive, satisfied, and free. Paul is being transformed inwardly by a complete change of mind with the truth: God approves of me.

Listening for Truth

1. As you consider your images of God, do you see where there might be an internal conflict between what you theologically believe and what you internally experience?
2. Picture God looking at you—what expression do you see on His face as His eyes meet yours?
3. Reflect on the statement, "He created me just like He wants me for a specific purpose." Talk with God and share your feelings about this idea.
4. Think over the possibility that you might have a root lie that God doesn't approve of me. What kind of thoughts could be feeding that lie? What does that berry look like?

Chapter 17

THE ROOT LIE: GOD IS NOT IN CONTROL

My teenage daughter caught me in the kitchen, standing outside the pantry, talking to myself. She noticed my worried look and asked if everything was OK. "Sure!" I responded, but too quickly and too fake. She was on to me. "No, really Mom, are you OK? What's wrong? I can tell something is wrong." I was caught. Something was wrong. I had been rolling through my "what-ifs?" allowing my mind to bring me to that anxious place. That place where I feel like if God is not going to do something about my situation, then maybe I should help Him out. I don't like waiting. I was so anxious and needed to hear from Him, but no answer. I felt a huge heaviness. I had nothing to say to respond to her.

My thoughts raced, "This is real, God. What do I believe about You? Do I believe you are in control? Do I believe that You are good? Do I believe that You are right here with me? Or do I just say that I do? Will I justify my worry and continue in anxiety, showing my daughter that You are not truly in control? Or will I continue trying to fake it? This is a chance to live out what I say I believe, even when I don't feel it. Honestly, all the things I worry about come down to what I believe about you, God." I take a deep breath and tell her the truth, that I am fighting a battle in my mind and struggling to believe that God is in control.

We pray, and I hug her. Just saying it out loud and confessing it had helped me realize the power I was giving that ugly lie. Not today . . . the lie that God is not in control is not going to get any publicity from me. I am no longer in that rut. I am on my way to excavating that ugly lie and replacing it with the solid truth that God is in control. Later, I came across this Bible verse that made me smile. This is what I will speak to myself when I feel like I have been waiting too long for God to do something and give in to the lie that God is not really in control.

> *I waited and waited and waited for God. At last, he looked; finally he listened. He lifted me out of the ditch, pulled me from deep mud. He stood me up on a solid rock to make sure I wouldn't slip. He taught me how to sing the latest God-song, a praise-song to our God.*
>
> —Psalm 40:1–3 MSG

I will no longer be promoting the lie. Rather, I will be singing praises to God, reminding myself of the truth, God **is** in control. Here is a look at the conversation in my head as I worked from my berry of "fear of the future" to get down to my root lie that "God is not in control." It went something like this:

Inner voice: Why am I feeling so anxious?

Me: Because I don't know what else to do.

Inner voice: Why do I feel like I should do something?

Me: Because I'm just waiting, and it seems like I should be doing something.

Inner voice: Why do I feel like that?

Me: By doing something, I would feel some control.

Inner voice: Why do I feel like I need control?

Me: I want to be in control. I need certain things to happen just like I think they should.

Inner voice: Why?

Me: I need things to be tied up in a pretty bow. I don't feel like that is going to happen, Truthfully, I'd like my way, it seems best.

Inner voice: Why?

Me: God isn't doing anything. I don't believe God has a plan.

Inner voice: Why do I feel like that?

Me: I don't believe that God is truly in control.

I found my root lie: God is not in control. When I realized the root lie of my anxiety, I saw the absurdity of my thoughts. Of course, God is in control. That is my theological conviction, but why am I experiencing such a different assumption in my thoughts?

Figure 6. Berry Bush: God Is Not in Control

I Want Control

For me, the most obvious realization of my inability to control life appeared with the birth of our first child. Since that day, one of my biggest berries on my bush is worrying about my children's safety and health. This is a natural concern. We want to protect them. That is why many parents struggle with the tendency to be "helicopter parents." As a new parent, I realized quickly that although I wanted to control this child, it was impossible. Meal times were the epitome of my trying to control what the baby ate and when he ate, but he decided when he would open his mouth and if he would swallow it or spit it out. This little human had his own ideas about what he wanted to do and when he wanted to do it. Slowly, it began to dawn on me that all my attempts at control were an illusion. Despite all my efforts, it was ultimately up to him to decide for himself. This desire for control doesn't stop as our child grows. We love them and want what is best for them, but they are the ones choosing their own journey. They will have to navigate their life their way; however, as they do, we stand on the sidelines cheering them on, watching, waiting to see how we can "help God," and wishing we could control their environment or their responses at least. This feeling drives us to our knees in utter desperation.

Although I'm referring here to the desire to control my kids, that is not all that I want to control. My desire for control runs the full gamut of every part of my life. From my relationships to the weather, I want to try to figure things out so that I do not have to incur pain of any kind. I want my way. Self is telling me that it is the best way. All humans struggle with control because, just like Eve, we want to be God. When our lives are running smoothly, we are duped into thinking we are in control. But the truth is, we're always one unexpected moment away from being reminded that we are not. Everything can seem fine right up until the instant it isn't. One phone call, one diagnosis, one crisis, and suddenly the truth hits like a jolt: We were never in charge. What felt solid was only a façade, a comforting lie the Deceiver is all too eager for us to believe. We were never in the driver's seat; we only thought we were. When we comprehend this, we have three choices: Accuse God of intentionally hurting us, give in to the lie that God is not in control, or trust in His character.

Anxiety originates from that desire to control. It is based on the fear of what might happen, the unknown. This is where self really shines. Our "Me Motivation" appears, and our desire for control comes out in ways such as micromanaging, excessively involving ourselves in others' lives, exhaustive planning, perfectionism, resistance to change, defensiveness, and more. Often, we are guilty of manipulation. I used to jokingly attempt to explain away my tendency to control my husband as "I am just trying to help you!" He didn't see it that way and now, neither do I. Now, I recognize it. It is my pride that craves control. Self tells me that I can define good and evil, what is best for me. Self wants my life to revolve around me and my desires. In my quest for peace, safety, and comfort, my own heart is deceiving me (Jeremiah 17:9). I am not God. I must trust that He knows what is best. This reasoning makes sense when life is going smoothly, but in the face of tragedy, it feels hollow. The expression, "God's got it," sounds trite.

Si Dios Quiere

When I was in my early twenties, one of my first jobs was working at a mission that helped those in dire circumstances with food and clothing. Many of the people that I worked with were Spanish-speaking.

They were so kind, generous, and full of grace with my inept Spanish. I learned many things from them, like how to cook, speak Spanish, and trust God. One expression that at first really bothered me was "*Si Dios quiere*," which means, "God willing." I had heard my mom use a similar expression, "Lord willing and the creek don't rise." Her expression seemed more like, "I hope nothing goes wrong to throw off my plans." However, when I literally translated "*Si Dios quiere*" to English, the words "If God wants" made me stop in my tracks. Although I believed it. . . . I didn't want to have to acknowledge that every single event I considered or planned would happen "*Si Dios quiere*." In fact, it flustered me because I felt like no one would commit to anything with a "Yes, I will be there!" When I asked, "See you Monday for Bible Study?" The response would typically be, "*Si Dios quiere*." Of course, with time and more cultural experience, I realized any phrase referring to the future always had this added to it at the end.

Eventually, "*Si Dios quiere*" began to come off my own lips as well, with more of the connotation of "hopefully." Spanish has several expressions that reference God's sovereignty like "*Dios mediante*" and "*Si Dios lo permite*." They are all ways of acknowledging God is in control, but of course Spanish is not the only language that has these kinds of expressions. Although it has been a long time since I thought about that time and the expression "*Si Dios quiere*," I was recently reminded of it when I heard a story about the same phrase in Arabic, "*Inshallah*," being used by two students. They were good friends. One was American from the Midwest, and the other was a devout Muslim from the Middle East. After an afternoon of studying together, they said their goodbyes. The American reminded the Muslim, "We will meet up tomorrow at the library at noon." The Muslim friend said nothing. So, the American repeated himself, thinking he hadn't heard him, he tapped his friend on the shoulder. His friend turned to him and ordered, "Say *Inshallah*." In a lighthearted way, the American laughed and responded, "OK. OK. *Inshallah*." His friend's eyes were kind, but his tone was serious, and his voice was stern, "You are so arrogant. You think you are in control of everything, but you are not. You don't know what could happen. A car could hit you. You could slip in the tub and hit your head, suffer a heart attack, or something else might change all your plans. God is in charge, not you!" This admonishment came from his Muslim friend, but it is biblical. The Bible warns us in James 4:13–15 against the arrogance of believing that we are masters of our own fate. Our problem is that we have no control over time or the events in our brief and temporary lives. It reminds us to trust His character. He is sovereign and working everything out for His glory. The idea that God's got it, or adding "*Si Dios quiere*" to our plans, no longer seems cliché to me.

Confronting the Wall

"I just trust Your sovereign hand," my friend prayed as a possible cancer diagnosis hung in the air. I was on the phone, praying with her as she filled me in on the news she had just gotten from the doctor. How could she pray this way when it seemed as if her life was spinning out of control? She trusts in His character. She has learned that the verse "*Blessed are those who mourn for they will be comforted*" (Matthew 5:4) means that the blessing is that Jesus is with her and her broken heart, weeping with her, giving her His superpower of peace, catching her tears, and holding her. She can "trust His sovereign hand." There are so many verses I could put here to remind us of God's character. He is in control. He created everything out of nothing! He made it crystal clear that He is in charge. "*I am the Lord, and there is no other; apart from me there is no God*" (Isaiah 45:5). He has absolute authority and power over everything. Then why do I even consider the possibility that He might not be in control? The answer—my "Me Motivated-Self." When things go differently than I want them to, I want to blame God. He is not in control, or perhaps He is just flat wrong, or maybe He doesn't even exist. When something happens, and our illusion of control explodes in our face, we are forced to confront the Wall. "The Wall represents our will meeting God's will face to face. We decide anew whether we are willing to surrender and let God direct our lives."[1] Pete Scazzero explains how the Wall appears in a crisis and shakes us to the core:

> It comes, perhaps, through a divorce, a job loss, the death of a close friend or family member, a cancer diagnosis, a disillusioning church experience, a betrayal, a shattered dream, a wayward child, a car accident, an inability to get pregnant, a deep desire to marry that remains unfulfilled, a dryness or loss of joy in our relationship with God. We question ourselves, God, the church. We discover for the first time that our faith does not appear to "work." We have more questions than answers as the very foundation of our faith feels like it is on the line. We don't know where God is, what he is doing, where he is going, how he is getting us there, or when this will be over.[2]

The Wall is a way for us to let go of power and control. As we journey with God, there will be times when a Wall will appear, and doubts and questions will surface. We will not move forward in our faith until we confront the doubt and confusion that our desire for control brings. The Wall will keep us stuck, not maturing in our relationship with God, until we deal with it.

> Although we deeply desire to give our will over to God, and even believe we are doing so, in truth, we are trying to deal with the Wall in the same way we have gotten through life—on the strength of our own will or gifts. We try everything we can to scale it, circumvent it, burrow under it, leap over it, or simply ignore it. But the Wall remains!"[3]

God is calling us to go through the Wall, using it to show us what is necessary to become totally His. We must stop trying to grasp control. FamilyLife Today Radio talk show host and speaker Ann Wilson acted out the way we handle our desire for control. She, along with her husband, Dave, pretended to ride a tandem bike. Ann started off at the handlebars, with Dave playing Jesus behind her. She tried to steer it herself, but realized that Jesus loves her so much that she decided to trust Him and put Him in the driver's seat. After a while, she began to wonder, "Why are we going down this road? I don't want to go this way." She felt uncomfortable, so she began to backseat drive and tried to tell Jesus where to steer the bike. Bit by bit, she began to stand up on her seat in the back and point over Jesus's shoulder to indicate which way He should go. She ultimately crawled on top of Him, desperately reaching for the handlebars, telling Him she wanted to help Him. She was obviously scared and grasping for control. Check out the video.[4] It is humorous to see it acted out, it shows how absurd it when we grapple with Jesus for control. He is telling her, "Trust me! Let me take you where I know you will find joy and fulfillment." She shares about those moments when we can't look, just hold tight to Jesus with our arms around

Him and can't even pedal, but boldly asserts that the best place to be is in the back seat because it is "the safest, most wonderful place we could ever be."[5]

The Relationship Between Pride and Worry

Today, I was scrolling on my phone and came across a short video of Tim Keller addressing the topic of control. He laid it out so clearly:

> Most of us actually feel like we know better than God how our life ought to go. If it is not going right, we get anxious, filled with self-pity, we get scornful, we get skeptical, we get hard and cynical. But actually, patience and the ability to not worry and not be really upset when things are going wrong in your life is essentially a kind of humility. You know why? It takes humility to say well I thought this is how my life ought to go, but I don't know. How do I know?[6]

When I can accept that I do not know better than God how my life ought to go, I will have passed through the Wall. No more cursing God, questioning His motives, or even His existence, but to get through the Wall, I will have to fight the battle of humility. As I stand in front of my wall and consider it, my "Me Motivated-Self" will emerge, and with it pride and its best friends fear and worry. Keller's words made so much sense to me:

> It takes pride to be worried. It takes a lot of pride to say, "I know how my life ought to go, and I'm afraid God's not going to get it right." Humility is what says, "Well,

> I thought this was what really should be happening, but I don't know."[7]

One needs humility to pass through the Wall. However, pride gets us stuck and keeps us from moving through the Wall. It is pride that is feeding the root lie that because my life is not turning out like I think it should, God is not in control. It leads us to an empty hopelessness where we can sit and stay, blaming, accusing, frustrated, and alone, or we can remember that as believers in Jesus Christ, we have hope! No matter what sorrow we face now, it is temporary. We have the promise of joy. *Weeping may tarry for the night, but joy comes with the morning* (Psalm 30:5 ESV). Keller put it this way, "For a Christian, joy is always on the way because the One in charge of us, of the whole universe is our Father."[8] Our hope is in eternity with our Father, who will wipe every tear from our eyes, and there will be no more death or sorrow or crying or pain. All these things will be gone forever. (Revelation 21:4) Joy is on the way because our hope is the knowledge that our Father is in charge, and we can trust in His character. We can trust in His character!

When we become aware of how dependent and fragile we are, we will uproot the root lie that God is not in control. We will escape our desperate pursuit of control, understanding that every moment is dependent on God, His mercy, and His grace. Because of this, we can look toward the future and say with complete confidence, "*Si Dios quiere.*"

Listening for Truth

1. When have you promoted a lie about God?
2. Think about the first time that you realized you were not in control of what was happening in your life. How did you react?
3. Have you ever been stuck at a wall? How did you work your way through?
4. As you consider the root lie "God is not in control," could there be a berry on your bush that is feeding this lie?

Chapter 18

HOW TO CREATE YOUR BERRY BUSH

My phone chimed with an incoming text. It was from a friend who was fascinated with the concept of the Berry Bush. After contemplating the lies about God he had permitted to grow and root down into his thoughts, he had found some real peace. Wanting to encourage me in writing this book, he sent me a podcast episode from *With the Perrys* and texted, "Check this out—Jackie is talking about what the Berry Bush does!" I was excited to watch and hear Jackie Hill Perry explain how she traced her fears. She started out by sharing that a few days before, she had received a text from someone with whom she had experienced a miscommunication or some kind of issue. Jackie immediately felt a reaction and knew she didn't want to engage in the conversation. She sensed that she needed to pay attention to her body and ask herself some questions to trace her fear:

> She began by asking, "What am I feeling? I'm feeling anxious.
> Why am I feeling anxious? Because I'm afraid.
> What are you afraid of?"[1]

By questioning herself, she realized that past interactions with that person had left her feeling bullied. Now, she was feeling afraid that she would be bullied again. So, she had to continue questioning herself to be able to trace her fear. "Then what are you afraid of? I am afraid that God isn't with me."[2] By figuring out that her real fear was based on a lie about God's character, she was able to be bold and engage in the conversation, knowing that bringing God into the fear, she could trust that He was with her. She went on to emphasize that at the bottom of our fears we will find "what we believe about God." Our fears are asking, "Is He with me? Does He love me? Does He see me? Does He care about me?"[3] These fears and more are producing berries on our Berry Bush.

I am impressed by how quickly Jackie Hill Perry was aware of her body's reaction when she felt the fear, and I love how she traced that fear down to her root lie, called it out, and began living in the truth. God was with her in that difficult conversation. That is my prayer for you as you think about your fears and the lie underneath them.

Look at us! We have arrived! Enough of my explaining what it is and why you need it. You have finally made it to the chapter where you will create your own Berry Bush. I have been preparing you for this exercise since you first opened this book.

Let's begin with a mini-review. The Berry Bush exercise is a way to open up and express your fears to Jesus as you uncover the lies about God you have allowed into your life. It is a tool that will expose your unbelief. Visualize a bush with lots of berries on it. On this bush grow berries that are full of poison. These things are dangerous! They are hazardous to have around. So, to keep the kids and animals safe, you go out and pick all the berries off the bush. It takes a while, but you are vigilant and try hard to locate all the berries and dispose of them. But before long, more berries have grown back.

You have to go back out to the bush and pick again. This time, you try even harder to get every dangerous berry off the bush, but once more, they grow back. Now, you are exhausted, but you return to the bush to pick them off. This feels like the millionth time, and you begin to realize how pointless this is. You will never get rid of the berries; they just keep growing back. These berries represent your fears and worries that you pick off and give to God, only to grow back. You pick them off again, but they grow back. You try to remove them, but no matter how many times you think you have gotten rid of them, another berry comes back. There is only one thing to do. Get rid of the bush! You need to get out your shovel and dig down deep to the roots to excavate and permanently remove this poisonous berry bush.

This process will take time and effort, and it's wise to invite someone to walk alongside you. Digging up deep roots is often easier and more fruitful when done together. Having a trusted community can be essential in uncovering the lies hidden beneath. We have been working on naming our berries, so you should already have one in mind. Remember that the berry symbolizes that fear that makes you break into a sweat, and as hard as you try to control and rationalize, it won't go away. You can't just leave it on the bush, and plucking them off is senseless. Stop picking the berries! You must get to the root and dig it out. This is arduous work. It is not easy to dig down so deep, but to get to the lie underneath your fears, you will have to ask yourself "Why?" several times. As you continue to answer why you are experiencing this anxiety and fear, you will be able to dig down through layers of reasoning. Your answers to why you are experiencing anxiety help identify your feeder roots. Each feeder root that you can think through will eventually lead you to your root lie about God. But the feeder roots are not the main root lie.

Just as Satan's first lie casts doubt on God's character, so will our root lie. It will start with the words such as, *God isn't* or *God doesn't.* The root you uncover will be a horrible lie that you would never want to admit to believing, but the sad news is that we show what we truly believe in the way we live. The lie underneath all our fears will eventually come down to something wrong we believe about God: "God isn't in control or God doesn't love me or God isn't enough."

I am not an artist, but as a visual learner, I found it helpful to draw a Berry Bush in picture form. On the following page is a blank Berry Bush for you to use, but feel free to do your own thing. Some people prefer to list out, make a mind map, or use some other kind of diagram. You do what makes the most sense to you. The drawing is not important, but the process is—so take the time to work through it all. Let's get started.

Step 1 – Before you begin drawing your own Berry Bush, take a moment and pray:

Lord, prepare my heart for some deep work. Open my eyes to see whatever You want to show me. Like the psalmist, I pray, "*Search me, O God, and know my heart; test me and know my anxious thoughts. Point out anything in me that offends you*" (Psalm 139:23–24 NLT). Reveal to me where I am spending time and energy worrying or allowing my mind to obsess. Attune my ears to hear your guidance and give me the courage to go there. Use this Berry Bush to expose my unbelief and blasphemous thoughts. Show me whatever poisonous berries I am allowing my mind to worry over, and help me to find the lie about you.

Now listen to how the Lord responds. He will reveal a berry to you.

Step 2 – Find your feeder roots by asking "Why?"

If you are like me, you will recognize that you most certainly have several berries, but for now, focus on just one poisonous thought. This will take time and hard work. This worry is not what truly bothers you, even though your emotions tell you that it is. What irritates you is what is underneath. The lie that is the origin of every worry you have is a lie about God. To get to that root lie, you will ask yourself, "Why?" several times, and each time you answer, you will have found a feeder root. The reasons why you have that particular berry will be the feeder roots that are underneath the ground and nourish the main root. You might have many feeder roots, so keep asking yourself, "Why?"

It can be difficult, and you might get stuck. It would be good to go to a trusted friend and ask them to help you talk through the "whys" together. As we have already discussed, going through the discovery process together can be enormously helpful. I suggest you ask yourself, "Why?" as many times as it takes to reach the root lie. In my experience, it has taken on average at least five times to figure it out, but it could take more. Be patient and keep digging. Notice that after you formulate your reasons for your berry (aka your feeder roots), they are motivated by self. Likely they will start out "I need, I feel, I don't," or somewhere in your reason you will find self.

Step 3 – Find your root lie about God

Keep going until you find your root lie about God. This lie will start out with "God . . ." It should not start with "I believe that God . . ." This lie is not a lie about you. For some reason, it feels better to us to not actually verbalize the lie. We prefer to soften it. But this lie is too serious, too severe, too offensive. Go ahead and express the lie as harsh as it sounds. It will feel uncomfortable and wrong to say it out loud. You will be embarrassed to confess it. However, once you do find it and admit it, you will be able to stop growing those poisonous berries. It is necessary to state the lie beginning with the words, "God does not . . ." or "God is not . . ." Remember, your root lie is all about God and His character.

Figure 7. Blank Berry Bush

Chapter 19

POST BERRY BUSH

Now that you have Berry Bushed your fears and uncovered your underlying root lie about God, name it aloud. Once you voice the lie out loud, you have unearthed it and brought it into the light. Verbalizing the lie is a powerful part in the process of breaking free. That ugly lie about God no longer has any power over you. From now on, every time that berry appears, you will immediately recognize the root and will call it out, exposing it for the lie that it is. This knowledge changes how you react when that thought enters your mind. No longer are you susceptible to its poison. You will not allow yourself to perpetuate this defamation of God with your thoughts. You will take your thoughts captive and remind yourself of the truth of who God is, but this will take practice. You will find yourself faced with this berry again or something similar and will have to root it out. But each time you do, you will get faster at recognizing the ugly root lie.

Right now, we will deal with the rut that we have created. We are fully aware that these negative automatic thoughts lead us into trouble. Dr. Lee Warren teaches that we can gain control of this harmful thinking by performing "Self-brain surgery."[1] We do this by taking a pause between a thought or feeling and our reaction to it. This way, we can determine whether it is true and needs a response or whether the thought is false and needs surgery to remove it. How we think can change the structure of our brains. Warren explains that functional imaging enables researchers to observe brain activity in real time. When researchers asked a patient to think about the saddest thing that had happened to them, they could see blood flow in the brain and the networks occurring. When they asked the patients to think about the best thing that had happened to them, instantly the colors changed, and different parts of the brain lit up. This research shows that our thoughts are powerful and can alter the brain's structural behavior. Warren asserts that we have "co-creative power with God to functionally change how our brain is working"[2] With God, we can change the way we think.

Our emotions want to have a say in this too and can work against us as we try to change our thoughts. Jennie Allen offers a brilliant metaphor, "Our emotions are not meant to control and lead our lives, our emotions are meant to be like a compass in our hand to take us to the places in our life where we need to connect, we need to heal, where we need to grow."[3] Our feelings are not something we want to stuff down, avoid, or ignore; rather, let's recognize that those emotions are going to help us discover the parts of us that need attention. To change, you need to welcome those emotions and ask yourself why you are feeling that way. Those feelings will point you to the lie about God that has infiltrated your thoughts and influenced your behavior.

Let's consider how that ugly root lie has been impacting you. Because you have been believing this lie, you have turned to certain things to soothe yourself. To really get rid of it, you will need to stop feeding it. Become aware of when you are vulnerable to feeding the lie. You have most likely developed some unhealthy habits. Perhaps you have reacted like me and have made excuses for being rude and hurtful to others. You have attempted to justify yourself. You most definitely have participated in negative self-talk.

Taking Our Self-Talk Captive

The Bible addresses our self-talk, telling us to "*Take every thought captive*" (2 Corinthians 10:5). In her book *Me, Myself & Lies*, Jennifer Rothschild advises us to "4:8" our thoughts.[4] She is referring to Philippians 4:8, "*Whatever is true, whatever is noble, whatever is right, whatever is pure, whatever is lovely, whatever is admirable—if anything is excellent or praiseworthy—think about such things.*" In her book, she compares her inner dialogue to a thought closet where she keeps her lies. She tells of a time when she was stuck on an airplane due to mechanical issues. The plane had been sitting on the tarmac waiting for over forty-five minutes when the pilot came on to tell the passengers they would have to wait at least fifteen more minutes. As she says, "I was pulling some things out of some dark corner of my thought closet that were ugly, ill-fitting, and making me tense."[5] Suddenly, from the seat behind her, she heard a little girl's voice playing the game I Spy with her dad. They played a couple of rounds, and then Rothschild explains:

> The little girl said, "Daddy, I spy something good." Her dad laughed. I figured he laughed for the same reason I did at her pronouncement. It was pretty hard to spy anything good in our caged predicament. "Is it a bag of M&Ms?" he asked. "No," his daughter chimed. "Is it your new shoes or your sweet smile?" A tenderness washed over me as I eavesdropped

> on their exchange. Their words cut through my complaining and frustration and reminded me to fix my thoughts on "something good." In that moment, I decided to "4:8" my thoughts.[6]

Rothschild began to dwell on what was true, lovely, and praiseworthy. She began to play a game of I Spy Something Lovely with God. Next time you find yourself in a predicament where your poisonous berry starts to bother you, "4:8" your thoughts and play a game of I spy something true about God. Think on His character and look for ways you see Him in your circumstances. "4:8" your self-talk.

Changing the Way You Think

Proverbs 23:7 says, "*For as he thinks within himself, so he is*" (NASB). We need to take this self-talk seriously. Neurologist Dr. Caroline Leaf explains:

> Unchecked negative thinking causes damage because it upsets the electrical chemical and quantum balance of the brain as the tree-like toxic memories grow—a negative thought such as toxic stress literally looks like a gnarled thorn tree in the brain! This can affect the way we see our lives, thereby impacting what we think, say and do, as well as how we feel physically and mentally.[7]

When you speak lies to yourself, you reflect those lies in every part of your life. Our inner dialogue affects what we think, the words we say, the way we behave, and even how our bodies react. There have been days in my life when I didn't even have the strength to get out of bed. I had no energy. The weight I felt was fueled by the lies I was believing. If you're anything like me, you'd never speak to anybody else the way you talk to yourself. The voice in our heads can be harsh, unkind, and relentlessly critical.

You are the DJ

Hurtful self-talk is self-slander. Our self-talk shapes us and affects every part of our lives. Think of self-talk like the soundtrack to a movie. Just today, as my husband and I watched, (I talk a lot in movies, especially in the scary scenes), I was nervous and commented on how dangerous it was for the main character to go into that dark room alone. However, my husband said, "No, listen to the music. This music sounds more like a discovery is about to happen." I relaxed and enjoyed the scene instead of tensing up for a scary jolt. We take our cue from the music. This background music impacts our experience, driving our emotions. It can fill us with tension or invite us to relax. What you think and say to yourself will determine your life's soundtrack. You are the DJ to your thoughts. Sometimes I imagine what my life would be like if it were dramatized in a movie. Not the big, important scenes in my life, but the little ones. Those times when I am all alone with my thoughts. I am my own music supervisor, deciding which music to play in each scene. Consider for a moment your own self-talk and feel empowered in knowing that you are the one who gets to choose the upbeat, cheerful, bright, "giacoso" playful music instead of playing severe dissonance, scary, haunting, suspenseful music for your thoughts. You select the songs to set the tone and the mood that will accompany your thought life. Take a moment to consider the type of songs you are playing.

Talk to Your Soul

The 1981 movie *Chariots of Fire* has an iconic theme song[8] that I often have playing in my mind in those moments when I feel like I am struggling to persevere. The slow, deliberate build-up to the majestic climax leads me as I talk to myself and harness my thoughts. The movie is based on the true story of two athletes training for the Paris Olympics of 1924. One of them was Eric Liddell, who was not only fast but also a strong follower of Jesus Christ who stuck to his convictions and refused to run on Sundays. The movie ends with his athletic triumphs, but after winning his medals, Liddell went to China to serve as a missionary. During WWII, he was helping in a mission hospital when the Japanese took it over and imprisoned everyone there. While he was in that internment camp, he developed a brain tumor. One Sunday, while lying in a prison hospital bed, he heard a band of prisoners outside playing hymns. He sent a request asking them to play the hymn "Be Still, My Soul." As he lay there listening, dying from the tumor, he must have been talking to himself, repeating these words:

> Be still, my soul: the Lord is on thy side;
> Bear patiently the cross of grief or pain;
> Leave to thy God to order and provide;
> In every change He faithful will remain.
> Be still, my soul: thy best, they heavenly Friend
> Through thorny ways leads to a joyful end.[9]

Three days later, he suffered a seizure, slipped into a coma, and passed away. Even in his final moments, the testimony of his integrity shone through. It is evident that his self-talk hummed along to the tune of the truth about God and who God is.

In his book, *Spiritual Depression*, the famous Welsh preacher Martin Lloyd-Jones explained the problem with our thoughts, "We allow our 'self' to talk to us instead of 'talking to ourself.'"[10] We should not be listening to ourselves. We should be talking to ourselves. The words in our heads are directing us. Are we listening to our fears and anxieties, or are we speaking the truth to ourselves? Lloyd-Jones goes on to explain, you must "remind yourself of God, who God is, what God is, what God has done, and what God has pledged Himself to do."[11] He urges us to deal with "this 'self' of ours—this other man within us. . . . Do not listen to him! Turn on him! Speak to him! Remind him of what you know!"[12]

The importance of positive self-talk is nothing new because the Bible shows us how to talk to ourselves. In the Psalms, the words "O my soul" appear as the psalmist encourages himself to continue trusting in the Lord. "*Why are you cast down, O my soul, and why are you in turmoil within me? Hope in God; for I shall again praise him, my salvation and my God*" (Psalm 42:5, 11; 43:5 ESV). In Psalm 103, David commands himself to bless the Lord with every fiber in him. He tells himself to remember God's kindness. There will be a time when tragedy will strike, and we will be so full of grief. Our *O my soul* self-talk will help us as we sort through our deep emotions. Although we will be full of sorrow, we can remind our souls of God's comfort and character, how good, trustworthy, omnipotent, and loving He is. We need to prepare our hearts today. Decide here and now on what you believe about God. Tell yourself that your wrong thoughts and emotions do not get to be the boss of your mind.

Determine right now that your mind will not harbor lies about your God. Jesus tells us in Matthew 22:37 how to love Him: "*Love the Lord your God with all your heart and with all your soul and with all your mind.*" With all our mind! We can't love Him with all our mind if we continue to allow lies about Him to remain in our roots. We must give Him control to reign and rule in our mind. Jonathan Edwards, the American preacher credited with starting The Great Awakening, created "70 Resolutions for Life" to guide his personal walk with Christ, which he reviewed weekly. I appreciate self-reflective questions, and so I recently downloaded a copy. Resolution Number 25 caught my eye. It reads, "Resolved, to examine carefully and constantly, what that one thing in me is, which causes me in the least to doubt of the love of God; and so, direct all my forces against it."[13] He knew. The tendency to doubt God's love is something we all encounter going through our minds. Even the great theologians wrestle internally with lies about God. We need to examine ourselves to see what is causing us to doubt God's love and His goodness, and ask Christ to bring His resurrection power to transform our thinking. Romans 12:2 speaks of being transformed by the renewal of your mind. The New Living Translation puts it this way: "*Let God transform you into a new person by changing the way you think.*" What would your thoughts look like if you let God redesign the way you think so that you lived out His truth?

Talk with God

I began the book by telling you about a time that we received a text that ignited my anxiety about finances. This is a persistent berry for me. I have allowed myself to get into a rut in my thinking, emotions, and behavior that have reinforced the lie that God will not provide for me. I have permitted this thought to linger, and as a result have suffered. However, now I realize that my anxiety berry of too little in the bank account is fed by the root lie that God does not love me and won't provide for me. By acknowledging that lie about God and recognizing that my thoughts, emotions, and behavior are guilty of feeding it, I'm able to stop, call the lie out, and decide "**No More**!" No longer does this lie about God have any power over me. I rejoice, but then I lament. I mourn over the fact that I spent even one second giving myself over to the lie.

After we name the lie, it is time to confess it and repent. We tend to act like worrying is not a big deal, but when we see what is at the root of our worry, we realize that it **is** a big deal! Worry is not about me. It is about God. I do not want to advertise that God is not faithful. I do not want to promote lies showing how untrustworthy God is, or publicize that He is not good. I want to communicate the truth about His goodness and faithfulness, but I have not always done so. I have been spreading lies about God. It is time to stop and pray. Talk with God about your fears. Repent and ask for His help to stop going round and round with this lie in your thoughts, emotions, and behavior, reinforcing the lie and creating a rut in your mind. Choose to no longer live as if this lie were true. Ask Him to help your unbelief. Pray:

> Father, I have spent so long tarnishing Your reputation with my unbelief. I say that I trust You and that You are good, but my thoughts and behavior have not shown Your faithfulness. I am sorry for living as if I believe the lie *(name your root lie)*
>
> ______________________________.
>
> Help me to truly excavate this awful Berry Bush with its horrific evil lie underneath. I repent of living in such a hypocritical and unhealthy way. Forgive me for allowing this lie to ruminate in my thoughts. Forgive me for basing my feelings on a lie about You. Show me anyone that I might need to ask forgiveness because of the way I have behaved in

response to this lie. (*Pause and wait to see if the Lord brings someone to your mind.*)

Bring your resurrection power to transform my thinking. Continue to reveal to me how I have been living out this lie. (*Pause and listen.*) Give me roots of truth so that the next time a berry appears, I will recognize it, call out the lie, and choose to think of You and Your truth. You, Lord, are truth, and You are good. Thank you for Your love and forgiveness. Thank you for taking the power away from my fear and replacing it with Your truth. Thank You for being my peace. Empower me to know and experience Your love, to grasp how wide, long, high, and deep it is. Make my heart new by the power of your love. Amen.

Listening for Truth

1. How did it feel to verbalize your root lie?
2. Think about your poisonous berry. Were there certain things you did to continue on that path and feed the lie?
3. Take some time to lament the fact that you gave time, energy, and sweat to a lie about God and kept a piece of your heart from Him.
4. Matthew 12:34 says, "*For whatever is in your heart determines what you say*" (NLT). How am I using my words? Am I building up or tearing down? (think specifically self-talk)

PART V

HOW TO LIVE OUT THE TRUTH TREE

Chapter 20

CREATING A TRUTH TREE

One evening during devotional time together, my family watched a video about the temptation of Jesus.[1] We talked about how every time that Jesus was tempted, He refuted the devil with Scripture. With each temptation Satan presented to Him, Jesus responded, "*It is written . . .*" His strategy for resisting temptation was to quote God's Word, and He knew what passage to recite to shut Satan down. This ability demanded that He wasn't just familiar with God's Word, but that He had hidden it in His heart. As a family, we also talked about how Jesus recognized the lie about God hidden underneath each lie and then debunked it with truth.

The types of temptations that Jesus confronted are ones that our enemy continues to try to use on us. It seems that we face a multitude of temptations, but Bible scholars use 1 John 2:16 to point out that temptations can all be categorized into three kinds:

1. The Flesh – when we feel like we have a physical need to be met and need it met now.

2. The Eyes – when we look at something and feel like we have to have it immediately.
3. Pride – when we seek power and fame for our own glory so that we can make a name for ourselves.

Because He was relying on the Spirit to lead Him, Jesus recognized and resisted these temptations. We can follow His example and stand against these temptations by relying on God's power as we take up His armor and saturate our minds with the truth of God's Word. By relying on His Spirit, we can notice our berries growing on our bush and recognize the hidden lie about the character of God beneath them.

Stone to Bread

In Luke 4, we see the Holy Spirit leading Jesus into the desert for a time of testing. God had a purpose for these forty days that required total dependence. Because Jesus had been fasting, he was hungry. He was weak, and the devil saw his opportunity. I've always imagined the devil physically approaching Him in some sort of bodily form, but maybe it was through His thoughts. The text doesn't indicate how Satan spoke to Him when he offered a quick solution to His physical hunger by saying, "*If you are the Son of God, tell this stone to become bread*" (Luke 4:3). That seems logical. You are hungry, so feed yourself. However, Jesus had made a commitment to fast, and now the devil is suggesting that instead, He should do what feels right, eat. Satan arrived on the scene just when Jesus had a need, and he tried to convince Jesus that there were other ways to meet His need apart from trusting God. We can relate to wrestling with thoughts of whether to give in and do what feels right when we are tempted to satisfy our physical desire. We want to stand strong to the commitment we've made, but we're tempted to satisfy our own longings. Satan tries to get us to think, it's not that big a deal, and that we should do what will make us happy. The devil wants to get us to focus on what we need, telling us that it is urgent, and making us feel that meeting our needs is of the utmost importance. He relentlessly plants suggestions and ideas about how this is our number one need, hoping to cause panic that we will not be satisfied. He knows that once we are anxious and fearful, he can bring us to the point where we are willing to do whatever is necessary to have our needs met. Then we will take the steering wheel back from God and essentially say, "Let me take it from here."

As Satan is convincing us to focus on our needs, he is also whispering lies to us about God. Telling us that God is not good, if He were good, He would provide for us. We see the devil doing just that as he not only tries to coerce Jesus to provide food for himself to eat, but he tries to get Him to doubt the character of God, not to trust that God will provide. He attempts to use Jesus's hunger to convince Him to provide for Himself. Satan did not want Jesus to remember that God was the one who provided in the past, but Jesus did remember. He shifted the focus off His hunger, resisted the temptation, and rebutted with Scripture, quoting Deuteronomy 8:3 as cited in Luke 4:4, "*It is written: 'Man shall not live on bread alone.'*" Jesus referred to the manna that God provided for His people when they were in the desert. God took care of them in His timing and in His way. Jesus knew that hunger was not His greatest need, and He wasn't willing to allow Satan to redirect His focus from His greatest need, the Word of God. Our true source of life, His Word, is our greatest need, regardless of what our mind tells us, or what is going on in our body or emotions. Jesus came to show us how to live a life of total dependence on God. He shows us how we should respond to Satan and how to look for the root lie underneath his temptation. Notice that when Jesus spoke the word of God aloud, it stopped Satan. The same will be true for us because God's Word strengthens us. Let's follow Jesus's example of using God's word when we are tempted to meet our own needs. When we do, we will remind ourselves of who God is, and with our minds stayed on His truth, we will recognize the root lie. Let's imitate how Jesus found the lie about God that was hiding beneath the temptation. Jesus pointed out that lie, "God is not good. If He were good, He would provide me with what I really need." God is good. Look what He did in the past. He will do it again because that is who He is. Jesus relied on the truth of God's character.

Worship Me and Have It Now

Next, the devil tried to entice Him with immediate gratification—not having to wait but establishing His kingdom now. The devil offered a shortcut. He took Jesus to a very high mountain and showed Him all the political and cultural kingdoms of the world in all their power and glory. He told Jesus, "Look at this. You don't have it, but You could have it." Perhaps the devil hoped to spark a covetous attitude through lust of the eyes and to convince Jesus not to be content with what the Father had given Him. Then he proposed, "Worship me, and all this will be yours. Bow to me, and you can take control on your own terms. This is a faster way to get what you want." He offered a way to bypass the suffering and sacrifice that lay ahead. However, Jesus rejected self-sufficiency and chose to do it the Father's way, knowing that for Him to establish His kingdom, He would have to go to the cross.

Satan tempted Jesus by showing Him that He could take control, and he uses the same tactic with us. We are all familiar with the temptation to compare and look over to see that the grass is so much greener on the other side of the fence. In that moment, we are tempted to take control and have things done on our own terms, in our own way. My thoughts tell me, why wait? You should just get it done. In that moment, I doubt God's plan and do not trust that He really is in control. My anxious waiting leads me to grasp for power so I can feel better right now. I see things in this life that are beautiful, and I want them. Satan comes along and suggests to me that I can have them if I want them badly enough. All I have to do is worship him. That is what I am doing when I run after the things of this world, striving to possess them; I am serving them. That is what I am doing when I live for the things of this world. Whatever I treasure, that is where my heart is going to be. When I prioritize worldly pursuits, selfish desires and validation, I am bowing down to worship those things, offering myself to them. When I do, I am essentially bowing at the feet of Satan.

As Jesus gazed down at all the splendor of the worldly kingdoms, He wasn't distracted because He knew that spiritual values were more important and trusted that God's way was the best way. The opportunity to have them immediately didn't affect Him, and He countered with Deuteronomy 6:13, which says, "*It is written: 'Worship the Lord your God and serve him only'*" (Luke 4:8). He prioritized worship of God above power, wealth, and everything else. His response included the idea that worship meant not only reverence but also obedience, serving only God. Jesus said, "No, I'm not going to fall for that. I'm going to do whatever God wants." Jesus was committed to following God's way. He recognized the root of this temptation, the lie underneath about the character of God. The lie that said "God is not in control, don't wait for Him, activate. Go ahead, why wait? Move forward and do something now to achieve significance because you can't trust God to come through." Jesus exposed that lie and replaced it with Scripture. He rested in the truth that only God is in control.

Jump, the Angels Will Catch You

Because Jesus was refuting him with Scripture, the devil decided to try to manipulate Jesus that way. He does the same to us. Beware! Satan is not afraid of it. He knows Scripture and will use it in his scheming with us, too. He used Psalm 91 to try to persuade Jesus. Taking Him to the highest point of the temple, he told Him, "You are invincible, just throw yourself off, and the angels will take care of you. Show everyone that God won't let you be hurt." Trying to appeal to some kind of pride in Jesus, the devil explained that this showy entrance would demonstrate to everyone that He was the Messiah. Why wait? Go ahead and get everyone's attention now. This temptation of pride didn't work on Jesus, but it is especially enticing to us because we desire to be admired, to have significance, to feel powerful, and to achieve success. The deceiver loves to appeal to our pride and will manipulate Scripture and twist it around to convince us. He knows that if we derive our sense of self-worth from these things, pride will take over. Feelings of self-importance and superiority will rule, and we won't realize it. Our confidence in God will have transitioned to our confidence in self. Temptation is all about getting us to look to self instead of trusting in our heavenly Father. Satan tried to get Jesus to take His eyes off God the Father and put it on His own abilities. Jesus, however, did not hesitate. He recognized the devil's schemes as not only an attempt to get Him to fall to pride, but also a temptation targeting His emotions. He cited Deuteronomy 6:16 when he countered with, "*It is written: 'do not put the Lord your God to the test'*" (Luke 4:12). Satan wanted Jesus to test God's love. "If God really loves You, then when you jump off, He will protect You." The deceiver was trying to get Jesus to test what God had just recently said at His baptism, "*This is my dearly loved son*" (Matthew 17:5 NLT).

From the get-go, the devil had attacked His identity, and now again the evil one skeptically implies that He isn't really God's son, "*If you are the son of God.*" Jesus knew His identity, but Satan thought perhaps emotionally he was vulnerable, and he could catch Him there. Our emotions are open to attack as well. We know what God has said, but we can get to the place where our emotions get us to think something different about who we are and our situation. Our thoughts take us down a path that leads us to question what we know is true. Jesus's response shows that He would not allow His thoughts to go down that path and did not need to test God's love for Him. He already knew that God loved Him and He could rest in His love. Jesus knew the devil was a manipulator. He wasn't fooled by Satan's tricks and crafty attempts to lead His mind astray. He knew immediately that the slanderer was telling lies about the character of God and didn't fall for doubting whether God really loved Him. The lie, God does not love me, never took root in Jesus's mind.

Jesus's Strategy

As we fight off these temptations, let's use Jesus's strategy. He responded with Scripture each time. When you answer your berries with God's Word, you will strengthen your heart and your resolve to trust in who God is. Also, it will stop the devil. He will leave you, just like he did Jesus, waiting for a more "*opportune moment.*" Jesus had Scripture right there in His heart and on His tongue, ready to use it. How can we have God's Word available to us when we need it? Many resources are available to make memorizing and meditating on Scripture easier.[2] Scripture memory coach and author Josh Summers encourages us in his book *Memorize What Matters*. He became convinced of the importance of memorizing Scripture after a frightening encounter with police while living in China. He had taken his camera to a religious festival when officers suddenly grabbed him, pushed him into a van, and transported him to a police station. Sitting alone in the interrogation room, fear surged. He prayed and tried to recall every verse he knew. Without a Bible or device, all he had was his memory, and he could only bring to mind about twenty verses. He found himself wondering whether those few passages would be enough to steady his faith if he were held indefinitely. Summers confesses, "Why hadn't I been more intentional about internalizing God's Word? This sobering moment in the basement of a Chinese police station was the exact moment I decided to make memorizing the Bible a priority."[3]

When we commit Scripture to memory, we carry it with us wherever we go—through anxious moments, tempting situations, and seasons of uncertainty. God's Word becomes embedded in us, ready for the Holy Spirit to bring to mind exactly what we need, precisely when we need it. Over time, it shapes our vocabulary and becomes life-giving truth we can offer to others who are hurting. We need to internalize His Word. When we do, we allow God's Word to shape our thoughts. And we know that it all begins with our thoughts.

We try to change, but our thoughts won't let us. The problem is that our neural pathway continues to lead us down the path of lies. Our behavior continues. We can't simply try to make adjustments to change the way we act until we get to the root, because the root is the problem. We have to dig up the root. In his book *Winning the War in Your Mind*, Craig Groeschel gives the scenario of someone who begins coughing a lot and finds out that they have lung cancer. They begin using cough drops to stop the cough. He explains, "Thinking I can change a behavior just by removing the behavior is absurd. The behavior isn't the root problem. The neural pathway that leads me to the behavior is the problem."[4] We know that we cannot just remove the lies and go on with our life, we must replace them with Scripture. It is how we renew our thoughts. We must construct other pathways that speak the Truth to our thoughts, feelings, and behavior.

The time has come for us to replace that horrible Berry Bush with our beautiful Truth Tree. This Truth Tree is rooted in the truth of who God is, with verses that will remind us of truth, and fruit that will display a life rooted in that truth. In John 17:17, as Jesus prayed for his disciples, He asked God to "*sanctify them by the truth; your word is truth.*" God's Word is truth, and He will use His truth to unburden us from all the lies we have let into our thought process. He offers us peace and rest, reminding us, "*My burden is light*" (Matthew 11:28). God uses His Word to powerfully cleanse us from within. His gospel message heals us from the inside out.

Step One: Replace the Lie with the Truth

Now it is time to create your beautiful life-giving Truth tree. Begin at the root. Earlier, when you drew your Berry Bush, you started at the top with the poisonous berry and dug down, but to make your Truth Tree, you will start at the bottom, at the root of truth. Take the opposite of your terrible root lie about God and replace it with the beautiful truth of who He is. That is the root of your Truth Tree. Here are my ugly root lies from my earlier examples that I can now change from lie to truth.

God is not good → God is good
God is not trustworthy → God is trustworthy
God does not love me → God loves me
God does not approve of me → God approves of me
God does not delight in me → God delights in me
God is not in control → God is in control

Step Two: Use Scripture Like Jesus Did to Create Your Feeder Roots

Firmly ground your feeder roots in Scripture. Just as Jesus used the Scripture like a sword to fight off the devil's attacks, so should we. Our weapon is the Sword of the Spirit, which is the Word of God. As I typed this manuscript, I had to laugh out loud because each time I tried to type *Scripture*, my fingers keep hitting the keys in such a way that the word came out as Scrip*true*. Perfect! That is exactly what I want to remember.

The Word of God is true. I need that truth to combat my lies and to build my Truth Tree. Think of those Bible verses that remind you of this root truth about God. These are the truths that will help you stay on track when your mind starts to wander back into that rut and the former ways of thinking. To reinforce your root truth, find Scrip*trues* that will renew your mind. Put these on your phone or on notecards. Hang them up in the places that you will see throughout the day—in your car, in your bathroom, on your computer, in your kitchen, wherever you will see them and be reminded of your root truth. This is the first step toward renewing your mind (Romans 12:2).

You also need to fertilize your root with input that will produce healthy fruit. Just as real trees need deep root feeding to provide essential nutrients and microorganisms to the root zone, so does our Truth Tree. When a tree's roots are properly fed, the results will show in improved flowering, increased resistance to disease, and increased ability to ward off insect attacks. With our Truth Trees, proper root feeding will provide healthy fruit, a design to keep us out of the ruts, and an increased ability to resist the devil so that he will flee from us. Take time now to find those Scrip*true* verses that will remind you of your Root Truth about God.

Step Three: Consider Your Fruit

The last step to creating your Truth Tree is to consider the kind of fruit your root will yield. Ask yourself how you feel when you live out the truth.

Figure 8. God Is Good Truth Tree

Here is how I feel when I am basing my thoughts on the truth that God is good. I think of words like *joy*, *free*, *comfort*, and *peace*. Here are some verses that I consider root truths to help me remember that God is good.

- "*You are good and do only good; teach me your decrees*" (Psalm 119:68 NLT).
- "*Taste and see that the Lord is good*" (Psalm 34:8 NLT).
- "*But when the goodness and loving kindness of God our Savior appeared, he saved us*" (Titus 3:4–5 ESV).

Figure 9. God Is Trustworthy Truth Tree

When I consider the truth that God can be trusted, I think of words or phrases like *confident in Him*, *strengthened*, *reassured*, *secure*, *cared for*, and *at peace*. Here are a few Bible verses that help me remember the root truth that God can be trusted:

- "*God has said, 'I will never leave you; I will never abandon you*'" (Hebrews 13:5 ICV).
- "*Know therefore that the Lord your God is God; he is the faithful God, keeping his covenant of love to a thousand generations of those who love him and keep his commandments*" (Deuteronomy 7:9).
- "*God is not human, that he should lie, not a human being, that he should change his mind. Does he speak and then not act? Does he promise and not fulfill*" (Numbers 23:19)?

Figure 10. God Loves Me Truth Tree

When I live out the truth that God loves me, I think of feelings like being known, relaxed, held safe, not having to perform, free, and at peace. Scripture verses that help me remember the root truth that God loves me:

- "*How precious, O God, is your constant love! We find protection under the shadow of your wings*" (Psalm 36:7 GNT).
- "*This is how God showed his love among us: He sent his one and only Son into the world that we might live through him. This is love: not that we loved God, but that he loved us and sent his Son as an atoning sacrifice for our sins. Dear friends, since God so loved us, we also ought to love one another*" (1 John 4:9–11).
- "*See how very much our Father loves us, for he calls us his children, and that is what we are*" (1 John 3:1 NLT)!

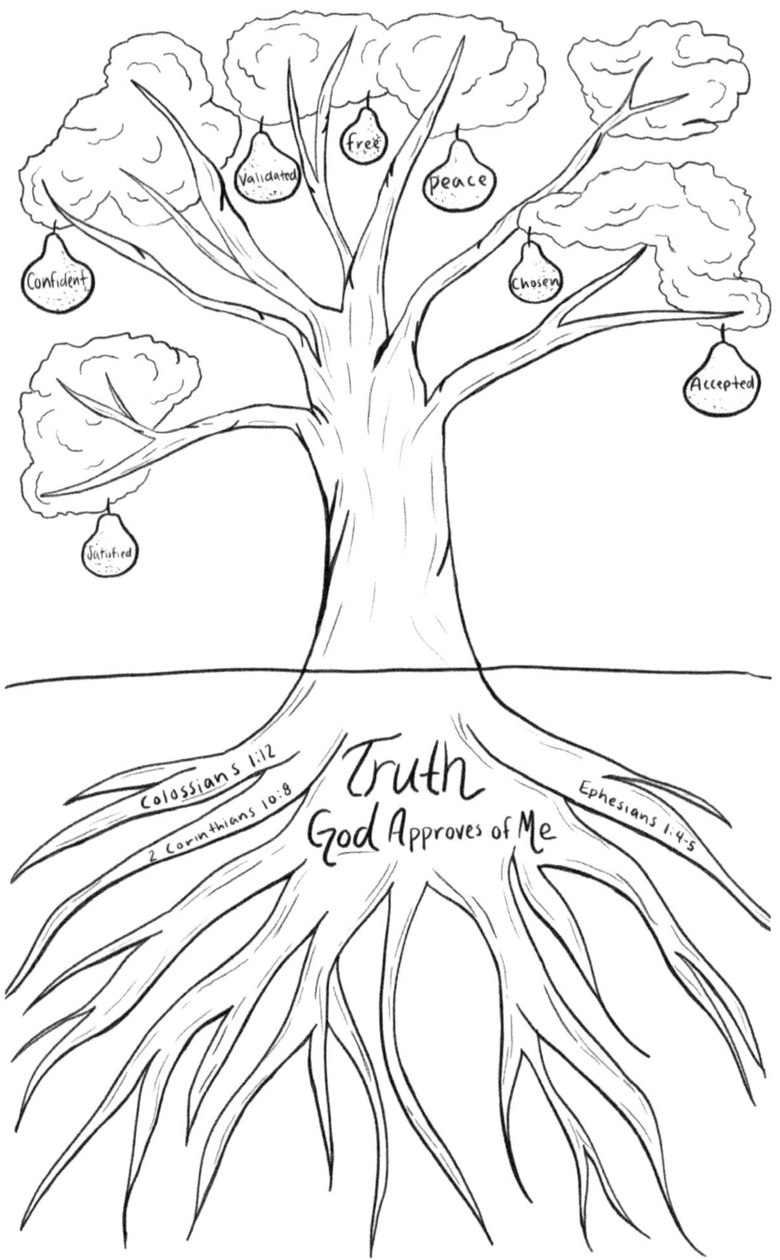

Figure 11. God Approves of Me

When I reflect on the truth that God completely approves of me, words like *chosen*, *accepted*, *validated*, *confident*, *free*, and *at peace* come to mind. These Bible verses remind me of the foundational truth that God approves of me:

- "*Giving joyful thanks to the Father, who has qualified you to share in the inheritance of his holy people in the kingdom of light*" (Colossians 1:12).
- "*For it is not the one who commends himself who is approved, but the one whom the Lord commends*" (2 Corinthians 10:18 ESV).
- "*Even before he made the world, God loved us and chose us in Christ to be holy and without fault in his eyes. God decided in advance to adopt us into his own family by bringing us to himself through Jesus Christ. This is what he wanted to do, and it gave him great pleasure*" (Ephesians 1:4–5 NLT).

Figure 12. God Delights in Me

When my thoughts are shaped by the truth that God delights in me, I am filled with thoughts that remind me I am His beloved and highly treasured. In that mindset, I feel free, content, uplifted, and peaceful.

- "*For the Lord delights in his people*" (Psalm 149:4 NLT).
- "*With his love, he will calm all your fears. He will rejoice over you with joyful songs*" (Zephaniah 3:17 NLT).
- "*He led me to a place of safety; he rescued me because he delights in me*" (Psalm 18:19 NLT).

Figure 13. God Is in Control Truth Tree

Living out the truth that God is in control, my feelings are calm, safe, assured that God's got it, and at peace. Here are a few of my favorite Bible verses that remind me that God is in control:

- "*All the days ordained for me were written in your book before one of them came to be*" (Psalm 139:16).
- "*He placed his right hand on me and said: 'Do not be afraid. I am the first and the last*" (Revelation 1:17).
- "'*Not by might nor by power, but by my Spirit' says the Lord Almighty*" (Zechariah 4:6).

When we rest in the truth of the character of God, we will understand what Charles Spurgeon meant when he said, "The sovereignty of God is the pillow upon which the child of God rests his head at night, giving perfect peace."[5] All these examples of the Truth Tree share the fruit of feeling at peace. When we live out our confidence in the character of God, we experience His peace. We will know and experience His peace when we believe the truth about who God is, and we will live free. What fruits are on your Truth Tree? Take time now to create your own Truth Tree.

Figure 14. Your Truth Tree

Chapter 21

LIVING IN THE TRUTH

"Oh, boy! Oh, boy!" I can barely hear the words coming from my dad's lips as another round of tremors begins and the clanging of the hospital bed rouses me from the couch. The hospice nurse told us that this is to be expected; it's the normal progression of his illness. I step up next to the bed, grab his hand to hold, caress his shaking limbs, and assure him that I am here. He is not alone. I kiss his cheek, stroke his nearly bald head, and remind him that I love him. Slowly, the panic on his face dissipates, and he relaxes, closing his eyes. He begins to take deeper breaths, which eventually turn into his soft snore. He is asleep. I stand there staring at his face, taking in his features, studying every bit of him. I know that it won't be long before Jesus calls him home to Heaven, and I will be left here with only memories and photographs. I don't want to forget his bushy left eyebrow (radiation has taken the right one), his strong jawline, his constant five o'clock shadow, and his kind, beautiful blue eyes that typically sparkle with joy and mischief.

I sit back down, almost trance-like, with my eyes fixed on the wall in front of me. There hangs a wedding photo of my parents walking down the aisle sixty-four years ago. It seems unreal. How does life go by so fast? My phone vibrates, notifying me of an incoming email. Picking it up, I study my screensaver and grin. It is a photo of my little first-grade daughter celebrating 100 days of school by dressing up as an elderly woman. She looks adorable in a curly wig we doused with baby powder to make it gray, a thick sweater, and colorful reader glasses resting on the tip of her nose. The dichotomy of the two images strikes me. My ninety-year-old father is at the end of his life here on earth, and my little seven-year-old daughter is just starting out on her journey. Our time on earth is fleeting. James 4:14 says, "*You are a mist that appears for a little while and then vanishes.*"

The book *Every Moment Holy* has a liturgy for grieving, reminding us that death teaches us, "All we gather in this short life will soon be scattered, that all we covet will soon be lost to us, that all we accomplish by our ambition will soon be rendered as meaningless as vapor."[1] This brief period that we have here is too short to waste on lies. Yet all of us listen to lies and while away our time, squandering days, months, years, and decades believing lies about God that defame His character. The way we live speaks falsely about who God is.

God Is Enough

Sadness is overtaking me tonight. The immensity of saying goodbye to my dad has really hit me. He has been slipping away little by little each day, and now there is so little left. His body is succumbing to his disease, and our goodbye is imminent. I sit next to my mom in his recliner and hear her say, "I don't know. I just don't know." Translation: She doesn't know if she can make it through this pain. I share her uncertainty. I have been turning over this thought in my own head, "Is God enough to see me through this heartache? I know that I am not strong enough. Is God enough?" This root lie that God's not enough, feeds all kinds of berries: fear of not being emotionally strong enough, fear of not achieving enough, fear of not having the approval of others, fear that you won't be successful, fear that you won't have what you need, so you are the one who has to work to get it. When we stand in front of that Wall feeling overwhelmed, this question surfaces, "Is this enough?" The thought, "maybe I need more," arises, and the idea that God is all you need seems too simple, too easy.

My dad stirs, and I squeeze his hand. He struggles to open his eyes and tries to focus on me. As I attempt through my tears to smile at him, I begin to sing one of my dad's favorite hymns. Although dementia has gotten most of his memory, this song remains on his lips. We "sing" together. His eyes close again, but his lips are still moving. The truth in the lyrics resounds in my heart, "Great is Thy faithfulness. Great is Thy faithfulness. . . . All I have needed, Thy hand hath provided. Great is Thy faithfulness, Lord unto me."[2] The ache still smarts, but the conviction that God is enough reverberates. All that I need, He will provide. He is enough. God is enough!

I love to play podcasts while I go about completing my chores around the house. Listening helps me get through them. One that I especially love is the *Ten-Minute Bible Talk* podcast. Recently, I was folding laundry when I heard Tanya Wilmuth share that from her perspective, our biggest lie is that God is not enough. I stopped folding and turned up the volume to hear her say that when we "truly believe that God has done every single thing He said He would do for us and in us, we operate from a place of enough—enough love, enough grace, enough time, enough strength, enough security, enough forgiveness, enough acceptance, enough."[3]

That is the truth that will transform us and our thoughts. How do we get to that place so that we can function from a place of having enough? We start by filling our hearts and minds with Scripture. Verses like "*My grace is sufficient for you for my power is perfected in weakness*" (2 Corinthians 12:9) and "*My God will meet all your needs according to the riches of his glory in Christ Jesus*" (Philippians 4:19) assure us that His comprehensive, limitless provision will take care of all our needs. God is enough.

I Live You

I just got a text from my mom, who is at the doctor's office, asking me to pray for her because she is feeling nervous about hearing the results of a test. I wrote back a prayer asking Christ to bring peace to her heart and mind, to fill her with His strength, and to give her the knowledge that He is holding her in His righteous right hand—she is not alone. After I wrote "amen," I added "I love you!" Rather, I should say I tried to add *I love you* because I didn't. The text actually read, "I *live* you!" Sometimes, technology can be frustrating! The phone had tried to help me with autocorrect. This happens to me frequently, changing *love* to *live.* It has happened so often that it got me thinking about the similarities of those words. When we love someone, we actually do "live" them. They are a part of us and have a part of our heart. Who they are is reflected in how we live. Our love for them influences the decisions we make, the sacrifices we make, and the way we spend our time. I *live* my husband by putting his needs before mine. I *live* my kids by listening to music they love while driving them all over town for playdates and sports activities. I *live* my parents by taking them to doctor appointments and helping them do things they no longer can do alone. I *live* my neighbor by taking care of her cats when she is out of town. I *live* my church by striving for unity in community.

I am sure you *live* your family and community much the same way. Our **love** for them affects how we **live**. In fact, I have decided to stop changing the word back to *love* but to just leave it as "I *live* you." It makes more sense to me now and seems so poetic. As we move forward with our plan to no longer live in fear and shame but live in the truth, let's consider how we say "I *live* you" to Jesus. Will we live out our new root truth? Will we live in that freedom? Living is abiding.

Abide

We have a tree in our front yard that needs regular pruning. Recently, my husband cut some branches back, and my son helped to move them to the curb. Somehow, one of the cut-off branches was left right next to where I park the car. The first day that I went out to the driveway and saw it lying on the grass, it was green and still healthy looking. The next day, the leaves were beginning to show signs of wilting. A few days later, when I went out to the car, the branch looked sickly. I don't know why I didn't pick it up and move it to the curb, but I left it there. The next time I went to get in the car, I barely recognized the branch for what it had been. The branch on the ground was dead. It reminded me of the example that Jesus gave to His disciples as they walked to the Garden of Gethsemane to pray the night before He died. Maybe He picked up a branch that had been cut off, like the one that lay there beside my driveway. Using the idea of thc branch and the vine, He taught them the simple truth, "all you have to do is stay connected to Me."

> *I am the vine; you are the branches. Whoever abides in me and I in him, he it is that bears much fruit, for apart from me you can do nothing.*
>
> —John 15:5 ESV

> *If you abide in my word, you are truly my disciples, and you will know the truth, and the truth will set you free.*
>
> —John 8:31–32 ESV

I have some wall art with the word *abide* in big turquoise metal letters. One day, my son pointed to it and asked me what it meant. I gave him an answer like, "Well, it means to remain in Christ—to continually trust in Jesus, believe His Word, and live for Him." That didn't exactly make it clear in his nine-year-old brain, so he followed up with a clarifying question, "What does that look like?" How would you answer? What does it look like to daily live out the idea of "abiding?" Most likely you have an image in your head of doing something like reading, meditating, and spending time memorizing His Word to describe how you abide. In fact, this is where a lot of us try so hard to "do" the abide thing. I know I have.

When I took a StrengthsFinder[4] assessment and found that achiever was at the top, I wasn't surprised. I know that I am driven by the need to do something. I derive a sense of accomplishment when I feel I have made some effort to complete a task, but how can I execute the idea of abiding? *Abide* is a verb, yes, but it is not an action we can physically see because "abiding" takes place in our mind. To abide is to surrender. It is an invitation to the Holy Spirit to transform our ways of thinking so that we allow His Word to fill our minds and direct our wills. We do not have to try to perform or somehow make "abiding" happen. When we try to describe abide, we use words and phrases such as *to dwell, remain, be present*, and *be held and kept.* Imagine yourself abiding. Think about what you look like when you allow His Word to fill your mind and direct your will—what it looks like to visibly exhibit belief. If someone painted a portrait of you in this moment, it could be titled "Abiding."

Abiding is doing life with God. While Martha was hard at work preparing a meal for Jesus and the disciples, Mary sat at His feet. Martha came to Him and complained about how unfair it was that her sister was just sitting with Him and not helping her. Jesus acknowledged how hard Martha was working and that she was feeling stressed out and anxious. He responded, "*My dear Martha, you are worried and upset over all these details! There is only one thing worth being concerned about. Mary has discovered it, and it will not be taken away from her*" (Luke 10:41–42 NLT). There is just *one thing* needed, and that is to abide with Him moment by moment.

After hearing about the sixty-sixty experiment in the book *Soul Revolution*[5] by John Burke, I decided to try it. This challenge involves checking in with God every sixty minutes for sixty days to stop, remember that God is here with me, and ask Him, "Is this what you want me to be thinking?" I started out strong with my watch alarm going off and stopping to check my thoughts, recognize that God is with me, and listen to Him, but there were times when I muted the alarm just wanting to go about my routine, saying, "Sorry God, I'm busy." However, this experiment truly helped me pause and catch my thoughts. I highly recommend this habit, not only to help you realize where your self-talk is going, but also to develop deeper trust, build a more responsive relationship, and simply abide.

Strong Truthful Thoughts

Look back at your Truth Tree. Gone is that poisonous Berry Bush with its dangerous lies, and in its place, you have planted a beautiful Truth Tree. By focusing on the root truth of God's character, we can keep our thoughts strong. Hebrews chapter six explains how to do this:

> *God cannot tell a lie. As a result, we can be brave and strong. We have trusted God to keep us safe with him. We should also expect to receive the good things that he has promised to give us. We can be completely sure about those good things that we hope to receive. That* ***keeps our thoughts strong****, because we know that our life is safe with God. It is like an anchor that keeps a ship safe.*
>
> —Hebrews 6:18–19 EASY (emphasis mine)

We keep our thoughts strong by fixing our mind on God's nature and promises. He is truth. He cannot lie. He does not change. That is why we can be secure in Him. Our hope in Him is like an anchor that holds us stable and secure. When you have the truth about who God is at your root, you will have His Word feeding and supporting your thought life. Your Truth Tree will produce nourishing superfood fruit that will bring you peace. Because you choose to abide in His Word, you will experience what it feels like to be free indeed. His truth brings peace that surpasses understanding and guards our hearts and minds whenever we are offended or when troubles come our way.

It will take time to fully live out the Truth Tree, just as our journey to become more Christlike. It is not instantaneous. The good news is that we are not alone in this endeavor. It is not up to us to muster the gumption to live out the truth of who God is. As believers and followers of Jesus Christ, we have the Holy Spirit. Jesus promised in John 16:13, "*when he, the Spirit of truth, comes, he will guide you into all the truth.*" We can rely on Him to teach us how to live out the truth with our thoughts, feelings, and behaviors. We come to Him and like the psalmist, we confess that, *"You know my thoughts . . . You know everything I do. You know what I am going to say even before I say it, LORD!"* (139:2–4 NLT)

We acknowledge that we need Him to expose our errors and omissions because He knows us better than we know ourselves. In Psalm 19:12–14 (EASY), David prays:

> *"Nobody realizes every time they do something wrong. Please forgive me for the sins that I do no know about. Lord, stop me doing things that I know are wrong. Do not let those sins rule my life. Then I will not be guilty. I will not have turned against you in a bad way. Lord, I want to make you happy. I want my words and my thoughts to please you. You are my strong Rock and you are my Redeemer."*

I feel like David in this psalm, urging God to intervene because even though I want to live out the truth of the Truth Tree, I know that I will overlook my own faults. I need His protection against my willful, selfish sins. Like this psalm, my desire is that my speech will reveal my love for God. Because of God's character and because of how I trust in who He is, my prayer is that even my thoughts would be pleasing to Him.

What Root Is Feeding Your Thoughts?

Christian scholar Dallas Willard was asked if there was a way to tell how your spiritual life is going. Is there a way to know how your journey with Jesus is going? The Pharisaical way would be to measure how often you are doing your devotions, how many minutes you are praying, and so on. I have measured my spiritual life that way, chiding myself when I miss a quiet time or something similar. However, Willard preferred to ask himself questions like these: "Am I getting more or less irritable these days? Am I becoming more or less easily discouraged?"[6] These questions reveal what root is feeding our thoughts. Is it our Truth Tree root or our Berry Bush root? The Truth Tree root is the source of peace; therefore, we know that the irritability and discouragement we feel must be coming from our Berry Bush. Check yourself; are you measuring your spiritual life like a Pharisee?

Jesus had a big problem with the Pharisees because of their hearts. He called them blind, self-indulgent hypocrites and compared them with whitewashed tombs, although clean on the outside, inside they were full of dead bones. He criticized them for being corrupt and insincere on the inside, pinpointing the problem to the attitude of their hearts. What about the condition of our hearts? Before we go any further, if we are truly going to live in the truth, we need to ask God to examine our hearts, to shine His light into every corner, to reveal anything that we might have hidden. Use these prompts to ask the Holy Spirit to guide you in truth and point out specific areas where He wants to work in your heart.

Listening for Truth

1. Am I doing anything that grieves or quenches your Spirit?
2. Is there anyone against whom I hold a grudge or carry bitterness?
3. Do I have any habits that hurt others or myself?
4. Using Dallas Willard's guideline, how would I describe my spiritual life?

Chapter 22

THE TRUTH OF GOD'S CHARACTER AFFECTS MY THOUGHTS, FEELINGS, AND BEHAVIOR

I could hear the phone ringing, but where was it? I had left it in the living room while I went to find my toddler in the kitchen, pulling out Tupperware. My daughter ran and brought it to me. I saw that it was my husband, Paul, and I almost didn't answer it right then because I was busy cleaning up. I thought, "I'll call him back in a minute." But my daughter had already pushed the green answer button and said, "Hi, Daddy." As soon as I heard his voice, I knew something was wrong. He did not sound like himself. All I remember really are the words, *accident* and *ambulance*. The emergency personnel got on and told me which hospital they were taking him to and where it was. I had never even heard of the small town. He was on a work trip and had left early that morning to drive up north.

I gathered some things, called my mom to watch the kids, and took off toward the hospital four hours away. As I drove, my mind was racing and going to all sorts of scary places. I was praying and crying as I flew down the highway, and truthfully, I was full of fear. However, when I turned on the radio, I heard a song about the goodness of God. The lyrics proclaimed how trustworthy He is, and I began to sing along. Soon, the truth of God's character changed everything about that moment. The truth about His character dispelled my lies. I knew I was no longer alone in that car. I knew God was with me. My fears were heavy, and the unknown awaited me at the hospital, but focusing on God's character and His truth carried me through those miles.

Psalm 34:4–5 tells us, "*I sought the Lord, and he answered me; he delivered me from all my fears. Those who look to Him are radiant; their faces are never covered with shame.*" A transformation occurs within us as we choose to seek the Lord rather than ruminating over our fears. He will deliver us from all our fears as we "turn our eyes upon Jesus, look full in His wonderful face."[1] Looking on Him, your face shines, and you become radiant.

I mentioned earlier about my walks around my neighborhood. The other day, I was struck by the beauty of the reflections that I saw in the water of the little ponds that I pass by. I lingered, gazing at the gorgeous reflection on the water, then raised my gaze to the actual image of green shrubbery and foliage. I was stunned to see that the bushes and trees were not nearly as pretty as their reflections. I kept walking and, at another pond, stopped to take in the reflections of different-colored condos playing on the water. In the reflection, they were breathtaking, but once again, when I turned my eyes to the buildings, they looked ordinary. The same is true for us. We are simply normal people, but once we look at Jesus, we become radiant, transformed into extraordinary. This transformation occurs not only internally but also outwardly; our faces will shine with the peace and assurance that His presence provides. Even though our situation does not change, as we look to Him, our attitude and perspective will, because He is good and trustworthy.

My Rights as God's Kid

Beth Guckenberger tells of a time when her recently adopted son forgot his soccer bag at home. He had a game later that day and had told his teammates he wouldn't be able to play because he didn't have his gear. One of his teammates texted Beth and told her that her son had forgotten his soccer bag. She grabbed the gear and drove to school. When she found her son, he was amazed that she had brought it to him. He never dreamt that was something that a mom would do. Because he had spent most of his childhood in an orphanage, he didn't understand the rights and privileges he had now as a son in the Guckenberger family.[2] John 1:12 shows us our new privileges: "*To all who did receive him, to those who believed in his name, he gave the right to become children of God.*" Guckenberger explains, "As God's kid, I have rights I don't fully appreciate and definitely don't always take advantage of. One of those rights is never to be afraid."[3] Wow! Take a moment and claim that right as God's child, never to be afraid. Let that sink in down deep in your thoughts. How does that make you feel? How will you behave now that you have claimed the right to no longer fear? She gives examples of how she lives this out:

> If a child is late, instead of worrying he or she has been in a car accident, I just say, "Not today, Satan. I will not give

> you one ounce of my thought life." Then I use this moment to pray for my kids' life and future. If someone I love gets a diagnosis I don't like, instead of being afraid for a future *that hasn't been written yet*, I say, "God, I'm so grateful You use all things and will be glorified in this story. Involve me in what You are doing . . . " If I can see fear not as my weakness but as Satan's trickery, I am quicker to denounce it and move on in God's strength.[4]

In God's Strength

When we see fear for what it is—Satan's attempt to put distance between us and God—we realize that it is just his subterfuge. When I comprehend that it is not me being a wimp and soft, but that my anxiety is a scheme of the devil, I will denounce it. However, living in that dichotomy of assuredness and angst is only possible when we rely on God's strength. His power is how we can move on. Radio talk show host Brant Hansen advises his listeners to "outsource your worry to Him."[5] Whenever we feel like we just cannot handle the predicaments of our lives, we can imagine God taking them from us. First Peter 5:7 tells you to "*cast all your anxiety on Him because He cares for you.*" As we throw all our worries on Him, we declare to the Berry Bush, "No more!" and proclaim the truth of God written on our Truth Tree.

"Fear not!" is the most repeated command in the Bible. Our Lord reminds us over and over not to fear. He is an empathetic God who is in the trenches with us. He is not unaware of what is happening in our lives. He knows. He is the "*Father of compassion and the God of all comfort*" (2 Corinthians 1:3). His word reminds us in 2 Timothy 1:7 "*For God has not given us a spirit of fear, but of power and of love and of a sound mind*" (NKJV). He has given us a sound mind! Other translations say self-discipline or self-control. We are no longer slaves to fear and slaves to our desires. We have been set free. This is where our work with the Berry Bush and Truth Tree pays off.

Instead of allowing our thoughts to get stuck in a rut and continue the cycle of thoughts, feelings, behaviors, beliefs, and back again, we can escape. We can quickly move from having the thought, recognizing it as a lie, excavating the lie underneath the lie, and choosing our Truth Tree. We speak the truth about who God is. We dispel the slanderous lie in a matter of minutes and are able not just to say but genuinely experience the truth of Isaiah 26:3, "*You keep him in perfect peace whose mind is stayed on you, because he trusts in you*" (ESV). His peace brings a sense of safety. The rest we experience in our heart and mind and the deep-seated sense of well-being we feel come from Him. His perfect peace is ours when we are rooted in the truth of who He is, Yahweh Shalom, the God of peace.

What Does Your Life Say About Who Jesus Is?

"*Who do you say I am?*" As I read Mark 8, I felt like Jesus was asking me that question too. I had my Sunday School response ready, but that wasn't the question He was asking. "No, not your words, but your life. What does the way you live your life say about who I am? When you are afraid, what do your thoughts, feelings, and actions say about who I am?" Jesus is asking all of us, "Who do you say I am?" How do you answer? I am still growing on my journey with Jesus, and for today, I hope my answer is clearly shown by living in a way that proves He is good and trustworthy. That is how I want to answer His question. We live to showcase God's glory. Our lives draw attention to His attributes and characteristics. Our lives display

God. When we live out the Truth Tree, we become an art exhibit that portrays the glory of God.

We began this book by looking at how our thoughts influence the way we feel, how we act, and even what we believe, truly, how they shape everything about us. My hope is that as you've read, you've seen how knowing the truth about who God is can change everything about your life. Through the process of discovering what berries are growing on your bush and thoroughly excavating the roots, you have exposed the lie about God that has been feeding all your fear. Now, go to your community—to those people who love you and will talk through your Berry Bush with you. Show them how you uncovered the lie underneath. Share with them the freedom that comes from realizing that all your fears have another lie underneath them, and it is a lie about God. That slanderous root was excavated. You will no longer live a life full of poisonous berries, believing the lie underneath all the fears. You have replaced that ugly, poisonous bush with a beautiful Truth Tree, and from now on, you will tell those poisonous berries that they will no longer be able to grow because you have replaced the root. From now on, your life can overflow with the freedom and joy that come from thoughts that lead you to live out the truth about who God is. No more lies about God! You will live out the truth about God, declaring His goodness, love, kindness, sovereignty, and omnipotence. Your thoughts and the way you live your life will proclaim, "*I will make your name famous from now on, so people will praise you forever and ever*" (Psalm 45:17 NCV).

Listening for Truth

1. Think about a time when you were afraid, but after hearing Scripture or a particular worship song, you felt different.
2. Beth Guckenberger declares that as children of God, we have the right to never fear. What do you think about that statement?
3. What does the way you live your life say about who God is?
4. How has working through the Berry Bush and Truth Tree changed you? Who will you share your thoughts with?

END NOTES

Introduction

1. Nancy DeMoss Wolgemuth, *Lies Women Believe: And The Truth That Sets Them Free* (Moody Publishers, 2022), 41.

Chapter 1: The Lies of my Fears

1. MaRynn Taylor, "*Lies of My Fears - Official Lyric Video.*" YouTube, June 11, 2021. https://www.youtube.com/watch?v=tU6YaHiSFvc.
2. *Groundhog Day,* directed by Harold Ramis (Culver City, CA: Columbia Pictures, 1993).
3. A. W. Tozer, *The Knowledge of the Holy: The Attributes of God, Their Meaning in the Christian Life* (General Press, 2019), 5.
4. Robert K. Brown, Mark R. Norton, William J. Petersen, *The One Year Book of Hymns* (Tyndale House Publishers, 2017), September 11.
5. Don Chapman, "The Story Behind: *'Tis So Sweet to Trust in Jesus,*" *Hymncharts.com,* June 1, 2024, https://www.hymncharts.com/2023/05/29/the-story-behind-tis-so-sweet-to-trust-in-jesus/.
6. Chapman, "The Story Behind: 'Tis So Sweet to Trust in Jesus."
7. Brown, et al., *The One Year Book of Hymns*, February 4.

Chapter 2: How the Lie Underneath is Affecting My Thoughts, Feelings, and Behavior

1. Chris Thurman, *The Lies We Believe: Renew Your Mind and Transform Your Life*. (Thomas Nelson, 2019), 14–16.
2. Anne Andrew, *The Behavior Cycle: How Our Beliefs Drive Our Thoughts, Feelings and Behaviors*. Upbringing: Elevating Family Happiness, November 29, 2020, http://www.anneandrew.com/blog/the-behavior-cycle-how-our-beliefs-drive-our-thoughts-feelings-and-behaviors.
3. Lee Warren, "Rewiring Your Heart and Mind, Part One – Dr. Lee Warren," FamilyLife, March 6, 2025, podcast, https://www.familylife.com/podcast/familylife-today/rewiring-your-heart-and-mind-part-one-dr-lee-warren/.

Chapter 3: The Origin of Our Lie Underneath

1. Timothy R. Jennings, *Could It Be This Simple? A Biblical Model for Healing the Mind* (Lennox Publishing, 2012), 29.
2. Wolgemuth, *Lies Women Believe*, 39.
3. Wolgemuth, *Lies Women Believe*, 40.
4. Kyle Idleman, *Every Thought Captive: Battling Your Mental Giants* (Thomas Nelson, 2024), 25, Kindle edition.
5. Idleman, *Every Thought Captive*, 25.
6. Marcus Warner, *Deeper Walk: Real Help for Real Life* (Moody Publishers, 2019).
7. Warner, "Dealing With the Wounds of the Past: A Deeper Walk Session 3," Deeper Walk International, YouTube video,12:18, June 12, 2025, https://www.youtube.com/watch?v=A3MsKbnhDlI.

Chapter 4: Warning! Dangerous Deceiver Ahead!

1. Beth Guckenberger, *Throw the First Punch: Defeating the Enemy Hell-Bent on Your Destruction* (David C. Cook, 2022).

Chapter 5: How to Stand Against Satan

1. Paul LeBoutillier, "Ephesians 6 (Part 2): 10—20 • Fighting Spiritual Battles." Through the Bible with Pastor Paul, September, 2018, YouTube, https://www.youtube.com/watch?v=VXCL3_akaKo
2. Jerry Bridges, *The Discipline of Grace: God's Role and Our Role in the Pursuit of Holiness* (NavPress, 2006), 137, Kindle edition.
3. Milton Vincent, *A Gospel Primer for Christians: Learning to See the Glories of God's Love* (Focus Publishing, 2008), 15–16.
4. George Duffield Jr., "Stand Up, Stand Up for Jesus," 1858, hymn.

Chapter 6: How to Stand Together Against Satan

1. Steven P. Wickstrom, "The Armor of God." Spwickstrom.com. https://www.spwickstrom.com/armor/.
2. Bailey T. Hurley, "*The Shield of Faith*," She Reads Truth, April 26, 2022, https://shereadstruth.com/the-shield-of-faith/.
3. Derwin L. Gray, *How to Heal Our Racial Divide: What the Bible Says, and the First Christians Knew, About Racial Reconciliation* (Tyndale House Publishers, 2022), 11, Kindle edition.
4. Auburn Powell, "The Importance of Studying Scripture in Community," *Radical*, December 15, 2022, https://radical.net/article/study-scripture-in-community/.

Chapter 7: Stand in Prayer and Be Flabbergasted

1. Patricia St. John, *A Young Person's Guide to Knowing God* (Christian Focus, 2014), 171–173.
2. Collin Outerbridge, "Fight Club Part 4: Fighting Words," Nona Church, August 31, 2025, https://youtu.be/WRC9pdO3UD8?si=opnEzxPwEjoC-kTR.
3. Philip Yancey, *Prayer Does It Make Any Difference?* (Zondervan, 2006), 143.

4. Paul E. Miller, *A Praying Life* (Navpress, 2009), 54.

5. Miller, *Praying Life*, 55.

Chapter 8: How You Put Out the Welcome Mat for Satan

1. LeBoutillier, "1 Corinthians 10:13 – Temptation and the Way of Escape," Through the Bible with Pastor Paul, YouTube video, 28:17, posted May 29, 2016, https://youtu.be/nclWmfFWJJo.

2. John Mark Comer, *Live No Lies: Recognize and Resist the Three Enemies That Sabotage Your Peace* (Waterbrook, 2021), 6.

3. LeBoutillier, "Luke 17 (Part 1) :1–10 • The Dynamics of Forgiveness," Through the Bible with Pastor Paul, YouTube video, 39:11, posted December 2, 2019, https://www.youtube.com/watch?v=ey_orrxaPOA.

4. LeBoutillier, "Luke 17 (Part 1)."

5. Lysa TerKeurst, "Inviting God Into Our Pain," Proverbs 31 Ministries, March 2, 2023, https://proverbs31.org/read/devotions/full-post/2023/03/02/inviting-god-into-our-pain.

6. Louie Giglio, *Don't Give the Enemy a Seat at Your Table: It's Time to Win the Battle of Your Mind* (Thomas Nelson, 2021).

7. *The Aesop for Children*, "The Ass Carrying the Image," Library of Congress Aesop Fables, Accessed September 14, 2025, https://read.gov/aesop/053.html.

8. *The Most Up-To-Date Pornography Statistics*, Covenant Eyes, Accessed January 3, 2022, https://www.covenanteyes.com/pornstats/.

9. Annie F. Downs, "Episode 328: John Mark Comer + Live No Lies" That Sounds Fun Podcast with Annie F. Downs (podcast transcript/PDF), September 27, 2021, https://www.anniefdowns.com/wp-content/uploads/2021/09/Episode-328-John-Mark-Comer-Live-No-Lies-That-Sounds-Fun-with-Annie-F.-Downs.pdf.

10. Jennie Allen, *Get Out of Your Head: Stopping the Spiral of Toxic Thoughts* (WaterBrook, 2020), 10.

11. Allen, *Get Out of Your Head*, 107.

12. Tim Keller, "Spiritual Warfare," YouTube video, 37:05, posted August 10 2015, https://www.youtube.com/watch?v=JcPlfM7w-ZE&list=PLpZLfPPM64L6Jq6BCPs5DHa6zz2j2TwOT&index=2.

13. Keller, "Spiritual Warfare."

Chapter 9: Satan Wants You to Call God a Liar

1. Jackie Hill Perry, "Message 3: The Truth About Ourselves." Revive Our Hearts, September 27, 2018, https://www.reviveourhearts.com/events/true-woman-18/session/message-3-truth-about-ourselves/.

2. Herm Edwards, "You Play to Win the Game," NFL YouTube video, 1:34, posted November 13, 2015, https://www.youtube.com/watch?v=AK7fEjrqabg.

3. Rechab Gray, "Corruption: Part 1," *New Creation*, April 30, 2023, https://newcreationorl.org/project/043023/.

4. G. K. Chesterton, *Orthodoxy*, The Project Gutenberg eBook of Orthodoxy, Accessed October 14, 2025, https://www.gutenberg.org/files/16769/16769-h/16769-h.htm.

5. Shelby Abott, "I have a New Name: Hosanna Wong," *Real Life Loading – FamilyLife,* October 20, 2023, podcast, http://www.familylife.com/podcast/real-life-loading/i-have-a-new-name-hosanna-wong/.

6. Hosanna Wong, *I Have a New Name*. YouTube video. 6:32, April 27, 2023, http://www.youtube.com/watch?v=0A_uXO3CgwY

Chapter 10: Anxiety Is Coming, It's Time to Make a Plan

1. Mark Batterson, "Learning to Take a Deep Breath & Praise God for Partial Miracles," *Ann Voskamp,* April 10, 2023, https://annvoskamp.com/2023/04/learning-to-take-a-deep-breath-praise-god-for-partial-miracles/.

2. Jonathan Waites, "Choking on Anxiety," *Corporate Chaplains of America*, September 15, 2016, chaplain.org/news/2016/choking-on-anxiety/.

3. Curtis Chang, "What Does Philippians Say About Anxiety?" *Bible Gateway News & Knowledge*. September 17, 2024, https://www.biblegateway.com/learn/voices/philippians-anxiety/

4. Steve Cuss, Faith Driven Entrepreneur, "Episode 237: Entrepreneurs Are Anxious People (with Steve Cuss)," *Podcast Inventory*, Audio podcast, February 15, 2023, http://www.faithdrivenentrepreneur.org/podcast-inventory/episode-237-entrepreneurs-are-an-anxious-people-with-steve-cuss.

5. Cuss, *Managing Leadership Anxiety: Yours and Theirs* (Thomas Nelson, 2019).

6. Brant Hansen, *The Men We Need: God's Purpose for the Manly Man, the Avid Indoorsman, or Any Man Willing to Show Up* (Baker Books, 2022), 178.

7. Debbie Hampton, "How Your Thoughts Change Your Brain, Cells and Genes," *HuffPost*, March 24, 2017, https://www.huffpost.com/entry/how-your-thoughts-change-your-brain-cells-and-genes_b_9516176.

8. Robert A. Emmons, *The Little Book of Gratitude* (Gaia, 2016).

9. Alison Cook and Kimberly Miller, *Boundaries for Your Soul: How to Turn Your Overwhelming Thoughts and Feelings into Your Greatest Allies* (Nelson Books, 2018), 9.

10. Chang, *The Anxiety Opportunity: How Worry Is the Doorway to Your Best Self* (Zondervan Books, 2023), 52, Kinde Edition.

11. Chang, *Anxiety Opportunity*, 53.

12. Frederick Howard Taylor and Geraldine Taylor, *Hudson Taylor's Spiritual Secret* (Benediction Classics, 2020), audiobook.

Chapter 11: Plan to Pray So That You Will Not Fall into Temptation

1. Tim Mackie, "Sermon on the Mount E24: Does God Lead Us into Temptation?" *Bible Project Podcast*, June 10, 2024, podcast, https://bibleproject.com/podcast/does-god-lead-us-temptation-lords-prayer-pt-5/.

2. C. S. Lewis, *The Screwtape Letters* (Macmillan, 1982), 28.
3. Mackie, "Matthew Marathon E33: Panic Attack," *Bible Project Podcast,* January 13, 2019, podcast, https://bibleproject.com/podcast/matthew-p33-panic-attack/.
4. LeBoutillier, "Matthew 26 (Part 3): 31–56 – Gethsemane," Through the Bible with Pastor Paul, YouTube video, 40:48, posted November 23, 2016, https://www.youtube.com/watch?v=7UPSwrY4Lfk.
5. Mackie, "Matthew Marathon E33: Panic Attack," *Bible Project Podcast,* January 13, 2019, podcast, https://bibleproject.com/podcast/matthew-p33-panic-attack/.
6. Ray Pritchard, "Deliver Us from Evil," *Keep Believing Ministries,* October 21, 2020, https://www.keepbelieving.com/sermon/2009-10-09-deliver-us-from-evil/.

Chapter 12: Plan to be Confronted with Lies About God's Character

1. Cuss, *The Expectation Gap: The Tiny, Vast Space Between Our Beliefs and Experience of God* (Zondervan, 2024), 14, Kindle edition.
2. Cuss, *Expectation Gap.*
3. Debbie McDaniel, "40 Powerful Quotes from Corrie Ten Boom," *Crosswalk.com,* October 24, 2024, https://www.crosswalk.com/faith/spiritual-life/40-powerful-quotes-from-corrie-ten-boom.html.
4. Anne Voskamp, *One Thousand Gifts: A Dare to Live Fully Right Where You Are, 1000 Gifts* (Zondervan, 2010), 148.
5. Joni Eareckson Tada, "True Woman '10 Indianapolis: The Stakes are Higher than you Think," YouTube video, 26:37, November 10, 2015, http://www.youtube.com/watch?v=RUYzGYmmFOY.
6. Eareckson Tada, "The Stakes Are Higher."

Chapter 13: The Root Lie: God Is Not Good

1. Matt Redman, *Blessed Be Your Name*, performed by Matt Redman, from *Where Angels Fear to Tread* (Survivor Records, 2002), MP3 audio.
2. Catherine Garrett, "Cathy Garrett: Amniotic Fluid Embolism and Stroke Survivor," *Birth Trauma Stories*, season 1, episode 2, March 30, 2022, podcast, https://www.birthtraumastories.com/birth-trauma-stories-team.
3. Christine Chappell, *FamilyLife Today* with hosts Dave Wilson and Ann Wilson, July 29, 2025, "Prayer Didn't Fix My Depression—At Least Not At First," podcast, https://www.familylife.com/podcast/familylife-today/how-to-process-grief-and-depression-with-hope-in-god-mark-vroegop-christine-chappell/.
4. Chappell, "Prayer Didn't Fix My Depression."
5. Chappell, "Prayer Didn't Fix My Depression."
6. Chappell and Mark Vroegop, *FamilyLife Today* with hosts Dave Wilson and Ann Wilson, July 29, 2025, "Prayer Didn't Fix My Depression—At Least Not At First," podcast, https://www.familylife.com/podcast/familylife-today/how-to-process-grief-and-depression-with-hope-in-god-mark-vroegop-christine-chappell/.
7. Vroegop, *Dark Clouds, Deep Mercy: Discovering the Grace of Lament* (Crossway, 2019), 28.
8. Vroegop, "Prayer Didn't Fix My Depression—at Least Not at First," *FamilyLife Today*, July 29, 2025, podcast, https://www.familylife.com/podcast/familylife-today/how-to-process-grief-and-depression-with-hope-in-god-mark-vroegop-christine-chappell/.
9. Vroegop, *Dark clouds, Deep Mercy*, 26.
10. Vroegop, "Prayer Didn't Fix My Depression," podcast.
11. Valetta Steel Crumley and Ed Erny, *Another Valley, Another Victory, Another Love: A Continuation of the Book Thrice Through the Valley* (OMS International, 2015).

12. Crumley and Erny, *Another Valley*, 41.
13. Crumley and Erny, *Another Valley*, 16.
14. Valetta Crumley, "*How to Overcome Pain in Life? A Christian Missionary Tells You About Her Life,*" YouTube video, 9:12. Posted June 8, 2025. https://www.youtube.com/watch?v=ZXqA_EreaKo.
15. Crumley, "How to Overcome Pain?"
16. Crumley, "How to Overcome Pain?"
17. Crumley, "How to Overcome Pain?".
18. Crumley, "How to Overcome Pain?"
19. Crumley, "How to Overcome Pain?"
20. Crumley, "How to Overcome Pain?"
21. Madi Anderson, "Another Valley, Another Victory," *One Mission Society*, Accessed November 8, 2025, https://onemissionsociety.org/story/another-valley-another-victory.
22. Anderson, "Another Valley."
23. Anderson, "Another Valley."
24. Jamie West Zumwalt, *Simple Obsession: Enjoying the Tender Heart of God.* (HGM Publishing, 2010), 55.

Chapter 14: The Root Lie: God Is Not Trustworthy

1. LifeKids. "*I Can Trust God,*" YouTube video, 2:11, August 4, 2023, https://youtu.be/t9NhSFi-a50?si=bB06z0AUQwuBXvAM.
2. Alexandria White, "77% of Americans Are Anxious About Their Financial Situation-Here's How To Take Control," *CNBC*, April 29, 2025, https://www.cnbc.com/select/how-to-take-control-of-your-finances/.
3. Stephen R. Adams and Gene Braun, "God Said It, I Believe It, That Settles It," performed by The Heritage Singers, from *God's Wonderful People* (1975), audio recording.
4. Allen, *Get Out of Your Head*, 39–40.

5. Thurman, *The Lies We Believe*, 44.
6. Chris Hilken, "Wrestling with Faith: How Pastor Found Hope in the Hardest of Times," YouTube video, 1:11:30, posted by *The Rollercoaster Podcast,* January 15, 2025, https://open.spotify.com/episode/1U80MZFmcwcJOolIPW3rmh?si=3f23f021581546f1.
7. Hilken, "Pastor Shares What He Learned About Grief, Loss of His Wife, and Ministry," Episode 3, YouTube video, 59:12, posted by *Faith & Culture*, January 3, 2023. https://youtu.be/QDkX7jZFl60.
8. Hilken, "Wrestling with Faith."
9. Hilken, "Wrestling with Faith."
10. Hilken, "Wrestling with Faith."
11. Hilken, "Wrestling with Faith."
12. Hilken, "Wrestling with Faith."

Chapter 15: The Root Lie: God Doesn't Love Me

1. Thurman, *The Lies We Believe*, 240.
2. "Matthew 16:24," *BibleRef.com*, accessed November 8, 2025, https://www.bibleref.com/Matthew/16/Matthew-16-24.html.
3. Dan Flynn, "A Spiritual Copernican Revolution," *God Can. God Cares.* July 28, 2020, https://godcangodcares.com/a-spiritual-copernican-revolution/.
4. Bible Project Scholarship Team, "What Matthew 6:33 (Seek First the Kingdom of God) Means." BibleProject, May 9, 2025, https://bibleproject.com/articles/what-matthew-6-33-seek-first-the-kingdom-of-god-means/.
5. Bible Project Scholarship Team, "Matthew 6:33."

Chapter 16: The Root Lie: God Doesn't Approve of Me

1. Juanita R. Ryan, "Recovery from Distorted Images of God – with Juanita Ryan," *The National Association for Christian Recovery*, October 2013,

https://www.nacr.org/abusecenter/recovery-from-distorted-images-of-god-with-juanita-ryan.

2. David A. Seamands, *Healing for Damaged Emotions* (David C. Cook, 2015), 18.
3. John Piper, "I Know God Loves Me, But Does He Like Me?" *Ask Pastor John*, Episode 1053, June 12, 2017, https://www.desiringgod.org/interviews/i-know-god-loves-me-but-does-he-like-me.
4. Piper, *Ask Pastor John*, Episode 1053.
5. Piper, *Ask Pastor John*, Episode 1053.
6. Piper, *Ask Pastor John*, Episode 1053.
7. John D. Hannah, "John Owen and the 'Normal' Christian life," *Modern Reformation*, November 1996, https://www.modernreformation.org/resources/articles/john-owen-and-the-normal-christian-life.
8. Piper, *Ask Pastor John,* Episode 1053.
9. Piper, *Ask Pastor John*, Episode 1053.
10. Sarah Kroger, "*Belovedness,*" from *Light*, Integrity Music, 2020, audio recording.
11. Henri J. M. Nouwen, *Life of the Beloved* (Hodder & Stoughton, 2016), 39.
12. Nouwen, *Life of the Beloved*, 40.
13. Jim Wilder and Michel Hendricks, *The Other Half of Church: Christian Community, Brain Science, and Overcoming Spiritual Stagnation* (Moody Publishers, 2020), 54, Kindle edition.
14. Wilder and Hendricks, *The Other Half of Church.*
15. Max Lucado, *You Are Special* (Crossway, 2007).

Chapter 17: The Root Lie: God is Not in Control

1. Janet O. Hagberg and Robert A. Guelich, *The Critical Journey: Stages in the Life of Faith* (Sheffield Publishing, 1995), 114.

2. Pete Scazzero, *Emotionally Healthy Spirituality: It's Impossible to Be Spiritually Mature, While Remaining Emotionally Immature* (Zondervan, 2017), 101.

3. Hagberg and Guelich, *The Critical Journey*, 114.

4. Dave Wilson and Ann Wilson, "Tandem Bike," YouTube video, 5:31, February 11, 2019, youtu.be/0Ak4TTvR0UE?si=3t0zmL-96LoJCHvH.

5. Dave Wilson and Ann Wilson, "Tandem Bike."

6. Keller, "Most of Us Actually Feel Like We Know Better Than God How Our Life Out to Go..." Instagram video, March 21, 2025, https://www.instagram.com/reel/DHeG5ttOo86/?igsh=bnBsb2J1c3hjcHY0.

7. Keller, Instagram video.

8. Keller, Instagram video.

Chapter 18: How to Create Your Berry Bush

1. Tyler Perry and Jackie Hill Perry, "Let's Talk About Boldness," *With the Perrys*, YouTube video, 33:21, April 14, 2025, https://youtu.be/yLbEWxnaF5s.

2. Tyler Perry and Jackie Hill Perry, "Boldness."

3. Tyler Perry and Jackie Hill Perry, "Boldness."

Chapter 19: Post Berry Bush

1. Warren, "Rewiring Your Heart and Mind, Part One."

2. Warren, "Rewiring Your Heart and Mind, Part One."

3. Allen, *Untangle Your Emotions Audio Bible Study: Discover How God Made You to Feel* (Harper Christian Resources, 2024), audio recording, chapter 4.

4. Jennifer Rothschild, *Me, Myself, & Lies: What to Say When You Talk to Yourself* (Harvest House Publishers, 2007), 44, Kindle edition.

5. Rothschild, *Me, Myself, & Lies.*

6. Rothschild, *Me, Myself, & Lies*, 44–45.
7. Caroline Leaf, "6 Ways to Quiet Your Negative Self-Talk Once and For All," *Medium,* March 14, 2019, \https://leaf-caroline.medium.com/6-ways-to-quiet-your-negative-self-talk-once-and-for-all-bb9a5133c90c.
8. Vangelis, "Chariots of Fire [Theme Song]," on *Chariots of Fire: Original Soundtrack* (Polydor, 1981), audio recording.
9. David McCasland, *Eric Liddell: Pure Gold* (Discovery House, 2001), 270.
10. Martin Lloyd-Jones, *Spiritual Depression* (W. B. Eerdmans Publishing, 1987), 28, chapter 1, "Spiritual Depression by Martyn Lloyd-Jones," accessed November 8, 2025, https://www.thetransformedsoul.com/about-the-book/chapters/chapter-1.
11. Lloyd-Jones, *Spiritual Depression.*
12. Lloyd-Jones, *Spiritual Depression.*
13. Jonathan Edwards, "The Resolutions of Jonathan Edwards, "Two-Minute Theology, accessed January 12, 2026, https://twominutetheology.com/the-resolutions-of-jonathan-edwards/.

Chapter 20: Creating a Truth Tree

1. Bryan Dwyer, "The 3 temptations of Jesus," *PursueGod*, February 19, 2015, https://www.pursuegod.org/thetemptation-of-jesus/.
2. Here are a few resources that have helped me to memorize Scripture: Awana program, dwelldifferently.com, seedskidsworship.com, thepsalmsproject.com, and listentoverses.com.
3. Josh Summers, *Memorize What Matters: 12 Proven Strategies to Memorize the Bible* (Next Step Press, 2023), 5–6.
4. Craig Groeschel, *Winning the War in Your Mind: Change Your Thinking, Change Your Life* (Zondervan, 2021), 85.

5. John Botkin, "The Sweet Pillow of Providence," *Magnify Christ*, February 27, 2025, https://magnifychrist.com/2025/02/27/the-sweet-pillow-of-providence/.

Chapter 21: Living in the Truth

1. Douglas Kaine McKelvey, *Every Moment Holy, Volume II: Death, Grief, and Hope*. (Rabbit Room Press, 2021), xxv.
2. Thomas O. Chisholm, *Great Is Thy Faithfulness*, music by William M. Runyan, 1923, hymn.
3. Tanya Willmeth, "The Biggest Lie You Believe: New Testament: Titus 1," *Ten Minute Bible Talks*, September 12, 2023, podcast, https://tenminutebibletalks.com/the-biggest-lie-you-believe-new-testament-titus-1.
4. Gallup, Inc., "StrengthsFinder 2.0," *Gallup.com*, November 5, 2024, https://www.gallup.com/cliftonstrengths/en/254033/strengthsfinder.aspx.
5. John Burke, *Soul Revolution: How Imperfect People Become All God Intended* (Zondervan, 2008).
6. Cuss, "Managing Leadership Anxiety: Yours and Theirs, S01E07 John and Nancy Ortberg," September 3, 2023, *Steve Cuss Words*, podcast, https://stevecusswords.podbean.com/e/s01e07-nancy-ortberg/.

Chapter 22: How the Truth of God's Character Is Affecting My Thoughts, Feelings, and Behavior

1. Helen H. Lemmel, *Turn Your Eyes Upon Jesus*, music by Helen H. Lemmel,1922, hymn.
2. Guckenberger, *Throw the First Punch*, 109.
3. Guckenberger, *Throw the First Punch*, 110.
4. Guckenberger, *Throw the First Punch*, 110.
5. Brant Hansen, *Brant & Sherri Oddcast*, episode 1854, "Mr. Chapman, If That Is Your Real Name," October 4, 2023, podcast, https://branthansen.libsyn.com/1854-mr-chapman-if-that-is-your-real-name.

www.ingramcontent.com/pod-product-compliance
Lightning Source LLC
LaVergne TN
LVHW010605100826
845148LV00014B/2854

9781632969705